8/8/1 C 12.95

◁ **W9-CPQ-124**

EKA 1

809
MCCULLOUGH

McCullough, David W
   People, books & book people / by
David W. McCullough. -- New York :
Harmony Books, c1981.
     p.   cm.

   "Previously published as Brief
lives."
   ISBN 0-517-54387-7

   1. Authors--20th century--
Interviews. I. Title.

PN452.M3 1981   809'.04 [B]
                    80-25842
                      CIP

Library of Congress
01932   n   596816   © THE BAKER & TAYLOR CO. 1155

PEOPLE, BOOKS & BOOK PEOPLE

PEOPLE, BOOKS & BOOK PEOPLE

David W. McCullough

HARMONY BOOKS, NEW YORK

For Ralph Thompson, of one generation, and for Ben and Katy, of another.

Inquiries should be addressed to Harmony Books, a division of Crown Publishers, Inc., One Park Avenue, New York, New York 10016.

Printed in the United States of America

Portions of this book were previously published as *McCullough's Brief Lives* by Book-of-the-Month Club, Inc. for its members. Published simultaneously in Canada by General Publishing Company Limited

Library of Congress Cataloging in Publication Data

McCullough, David W.
   People, books & book people.

    "Previously published as *McCullough's Brief Lives*."
   1. Authors—20th century—Interviews. I. Title.
PN452.M3   1981   809'.04 [B]   80-25842
ISBN: 0-517-543877 (cloth)
      0-517-543885 (paper)

10 9 8 7 6 5 4 3 2 1
First Edition

CONTENTS

FOREWORD

John Cheever first suggested that we go ice skating but then changed his mind and gave me a pair of hiking boots to put on. It was a sunny afternoon in January, 1973. Cheever's first short-story collection in many years, *The World of Apples*, was about to be published, and I had driven up to Ossining, New York, to interview him for what would become the first "Eye on Books" column in the *Book-of-the-Month Club News*.

We began talking at a dining-room table in the Cheevers' old Dutch farmhouse and then moved to a couch and then on to an upstairs living room. Finally, Cheever decided that we needed some air and began searching for ice skates. He found boots instead, and we headed out into the fresh, wet snow ("Perfect for snowball fights," he said) and on up the steep, wooded hill behind the house. We were both out of breath when we got to a toppled stone wall. "Mind that," Cheever said, pointing to a coil of barbed wire partially buried in the snow. "The man from *Time* magazine fell there years ago when they were doing my cover story. He has since died. No connection, of course." On the top of the hill, high above the unseen Hudson River and within earshot of an unseen highway, Cheever talked about the joys of singing carols on Christmas Eve at the local Episcopal church and how he suspected he was about to publish his last book. On the way back down the hill we carefully stepped around the rusted barbed wire.

The Cheever interview pretty much set the pattern for all the "Eye on Books" interviews that followed. I wrote about 300 of them in all. Although I usually prepared a number of questions beforehand, the interviews are not so much interrogations as conversations, and I found that a little silence often got a better response than a pointed question. I made notes of the conversations as they went along and never used a tape recorder. The more serious the writer, I noticed, the more distrustful he or she was of recorders. Cheever, for instance, would not have talked with me if I had wanted to tape him. John McPhee, I was happy to hear when I interviewed him at Princeton, believes that taping encourages lazy writing. As for accuracy, only one writer has accused me of misquoting, and that interview is not included here. Isaac Bashevis Singer wrote to thank me for "quoting correctly because others often quote falsely." But my favorite response was James M. Cain's "I have no direct recollection of telling you any of that, but all of it says things I have thought a hundred times." Notetaking itself rarely seems to bother interviewees, although one author kept asking me what I was writing down until I assured him that I was taking notes on what he was saying and not describing how he looked.

Getting writers to talk has never really been much of a problem, especially writers with books about to be published, and by the time I condensed my notes down to column size much more remained unused than was used. An exception was Tennessee Williams, who turned up for lunch with his agent and a representative of his publisher but in no mood to talk. I would ask a question, Williams would peer into his wineglass and smile, and his agent would answer. I think every word Williams said over that hour and a half made it into print.

A more common situation was one in which a writer wanted things said off the record. Often this came down to complaints about his publisher or his health. But generally the information was more solid. For example, Cheever, in that first interview, spent a good deal of time talking about his experiences teaching creative writing to black prisoners at Sing Sing (experiences that subsequently bore fruit in his novel *Falconer*) but insisted that I write nothing about it. Later I discovered that the Russian poet Yevtushenko had already published a poem about Cheever at Sing Sing, but for American readers perhaps a Russian poem is pretty close to being off the record in any case. Another revelation was James M. Cain's comments on Joan Crawford in the role of his heroine Mildred Pierce. He hated Crawford (which was not off the record) but thought (and this was) that Pat Nixon would have been ideal. "Her voice," he said, "is Mildred's."

My "Eye on Books" column appeared fifteen times a year in the *Book-of-the-Month Club News*, and there were usually three brief interviews per column. The subjects were all authors with new books that interested me and ranged from first novelists to

Nobel Prize winners to unsuccessful presidential candidates—three, come to think of it. There were painters, mountain climbers, ex-cons, a coal miner, film stars, cartoonists, a Mexican ambassador, an Israeli cabinet minister and poets from three continents. I conducted interviews in Oklahoma, California, Washington and a Brooklyn sewer, but most of them were held in Manhattan offices, hotel rooms or restaurants. A few, very few, were done by telephone. I have not updated the interviews in this collection, although I have added the year in which each was published.

The point of these interviews, these brief lives—if I may reach back to the 17th century to borrow John Aubrey's title—was to let the authors speak as directly to the reader as I could arrange it. If the book is to have a moral, I'd like to borrow it from Cheever. Years ago I saw him on a panel with James Baldwin and Philip Roth. Over the course of the evening Baldwin and Roth were asked all the questions from the floor. Finally, a woman—who I think must have confused Cheever with someone else—asked him why he wrote such depressing stories. Cheever pulled over the microphone and said, "For the entertainment and moral instruction of the reader," and then a long pause, "of course."

DWMcC
January 1981

x.

"I used to think that at some point you'd see your life as a long, narrative swing, that at some point you could see the shape of things and all the different strands would come together. Now I don't. You can find a plot to a week or a couple of days, but not much more, not to a lifetime."

Renata Adler was talking about her first novel, *Speedboat*, and how she worked away on it while waiting for a plot to emerge. The book is composed of a series of short incidents —some witty or satirical, some delivered with the sting of shotgun pellets—that record the daily lives of several New Yorkers who grew up in the 1950s. It includes two murders ("Both true and both unsolved," she says, "and like other deaths in the book they are 'by-the-way' incidents, the sort of things that come up in passing conversation"), visits to romantic islands that turn out to be not so romantic, scenes from the early days of the civil rights movement, and comments on subjects such as poison ivy ("It has no dignity . . . there are no poison ivy heroes") and verbal violence in reviewing ("The physical-assault metaphor had taken over the reviews. 'Guts,' never much of a word outside the hunting season, was a favorite noun in literary prose").

Renata Adler's earlier books were a collection of movie reviews (she was a *New York Times* reviewer in 1968 and '69) and a collection of essays reprinted largely from *The New Yorker*, as is much of *Speedboat*. "I couldn't stand my tone of voice as a reviewer," she says, "that and having to have an opinion on something new every few days. Reviewing just couldn't be a way of life for me. At first I enjoyed covering films because there is a news quality to them; they are events that happen in time. But everyone else seemed to take it all so seriously. Now I don't even go to the movies anymore—nothing seems to be happening there.

"I decided to try my hand at short stories because it is a

part of writing to write fiction—it's part of what a writer does. You have to try it no matter how it turns out. You sit down with something in your head, like a song that gets stuck in your brain, and you find there's a word that just has to be used to describe it that would be all wrong to use if you were writing nonfiction."

The finished novel, she believes, "is probably for '50s people. People in their late 30s and early 40s are the last group who remember doing things just because they were expected to by adults. There were still rules for everything in the '50s. Most people in the '50s who felt alone thought they were alone in feeling alone. To admit feeling alone was a sign of freakishness and, God knows, freakishness was a sign of failure. Failure was the great fear of the decade. I think the 1950s came to an end in 1963, when the civil rights movement gained momentum. It was something we could say yes to, and it was the end of our being hedged in by adults."

She is currently at work on a book telling what happened behind the closed doors of the House of Representatives Committee on the Judiciary as it prepared its case for the impeachment of Richard Nixon. She spent several months behind those doors as Committee Chairman Peter Rodino's speechwriter. Because committee employees were banned from talking with the press at the time of the hearings, she feels the public still does not have a clear idea of how the committee operated. "The most difficult part of working there," she says, "was the complete sense of distrust we all felt. If you knew something serious or important, you couldn't trust telling anyone. With such a huge staff you could never tell who was *really* working for whom."

Getting back to whether her book is a novel or a short-story collection, Renata Adler adds, "At first, no, I didn't think it was a novel, but then I realized that what I was writing weren't short stories either. There's a novel in there somewhere, so why not call it that."   (1976)

ALLIGATORS

Alligators, so the rumor goes, are alive and well deep in the sewers of New York City. Old hands in the city's Department of Water Resources believe the rumor made its public debut in an article by Meyer Berger in *The New York Times* during World War II. Since then stories about the beasts have popped up in a number of novels (the most spectacular being the underground alligator safari that takes up a lively chapter in Thomas Pynchon's first novel, *V*), and the city still receives enough alligator inquiries each year for its Environmental Protection Administration to keep on file a form letter that tries to lay the rumor to rest.

I suspect that when Harold Goodwin's children's book, *Top Secret: Alligators!*, gets around, EPA is going to have to run off a whole new batch of letters. Goodwin's book, which he also illustrated, is funny and a bit mysterious and a classic retelling of the myth: how baby alligators brought north from Florida as gifts from indulgent uncles are flushed down toilets by indignant parents and prosper in the warmth of the sewers.

After finishing the book I was all set to believe they really were lurking down there under New York's streets, so I made an appointment with Martin Lang, former Commissioner of Water Resources and now first deputy administrator of EPA, a man who has spent almost forty years in and around the sewers of New York and is said to know everything that needs to be known about what goes on there.

"Sewers," says Mr. Lang, an unabashed fan of H. P. Lovecraft, the horror-story writer, "aren't so bad. They're cool in summer, warm in winter and they're the vital life-support system of a city. In fact, the sophistication of a city can pretty much be judged by the sophistication of its sewage system." New York, for instance, has 6000 miles of sewers ranging from six inches to thirty feet in diameter.

And the alligators?

"Not alligators," Mr. Lang said. "Caimans. The things flushed down the toilets were really caimans from South America. People bought them in Florida, but they really came from South America."

Are they still down there?

"New York's sewers are the least glamorous in the world. Everyone knows about the sewers of Paris or Vienna or even Budapest. But New York's? Their only claim to fame is alligators. I hate to ruin a good story, but there just isn't much to eat in a sewer. There isn't enough to keep a rat alive, much less an eight-foot alligator. Sometimes I wish there were."

Before I left to see what a young woman from EPA's Office of Public Information said would be the Colosseum of sewers, Mr. Lang added, "Promise me this: when you write up this story don't totally debunk the idea that alligators are down there. Why should myths die? There should be some romance about everything."

The "Colosseum" was near Jamaica Bay, deep in Brooklyn, and we all put on rubber outfits and climbed down a metal ladder to watch a half-dozen streams of sewage, all bubbling as briskly as mountain brooks, join together and move off through brick-lined sewers toward a treatment plant. The place was cleaner than most subway stations, and there was not a bit of wildlife in sight. "If it flows along at more than two and a half feet a second, there's no smell," said John Flaherty of the Bureau of Sewer Maintenance. Mr. Flaherty also said that he too was a Lovecraft fan, and I began to suspect that the real story here was not alligators but the Lovecraft revival in the Water Resources Department.

"I was once bitten by an alligator," Mr. Flaherty went on. "Right here in New York." I reached for my pencil and notebook: an alligator story at last. "It was in the main reading room at the public library on Fifth Avenue and Forty-second Street. Somebody had a cardboard box. I put my hand in and felt something like a bee sting. When I pulled my hand out, there was a little six-inch alligator hanging on my fingers."

And what happened to the alligator? "I think someone flushed it down a toilet," said Mr. Flaherty.   (1974)

4.

YEHUDA AMICHAI

Just after the recent Israeli-Arab cease-fire, Yehuda Amichai left his army unit on the Mount of Olives and came to the United States to read poems from his book *Songs of Jerusalem and Myself* along the college lecture circuit.

It was the fourth war for Amichai, who at 50 is a sergeant major in the Israeli army reserve and the author of some of the most beautiful love poetry I've read. Born in Germany, he immigrated to Palestine in 1936, served in the British Army in World War II and has fought in all the Israeli wars since 1948. "My first encounter with grown-up life was war," he said recently, "and I think I used my poems from the very beginning to get over the imbalance between the reality of war and my dreams inside. It is a concentrated thing, poetry. You can carry it with you like field rations."

We talked about the status of poetry in Israel, and he mentioned a basic distrust of prose which he has noticed among the young. "They have been betrayed and lied to in prose, but you can't be betrayed by a poem." Perhaps because of this, he says, many young people have begun writing and reading poetry.

Curiously enough, Amichai says, there are almost no public poetry readings in Israel, which means that although he has read his poetry in translation to audiences in the United States and England, he has rarely had a chance to read it aloud in its original Hebrew at home. Instead poems are taking the place of traditional prayers in many kibbutzim. Amichai sees it as a healthy sign that poetry is maintaining its traditional function in society. "All poems," he says, "are really psalms: songs, celebrations and prayers."

I asked him if many Israelis are writing in Yiddish. He said they aren't except within isolated groups of Eastern Europeans and Russians. "But it is becoming fashionable," he says, "to sprinkle Yiddish words in Hebrew sentences or to mention having a Yiddish-speaking grandfather. This is something that has happened in the last few years, a fad, like having antiques in your house."

Amichai, his wife, Hannah, and their year-old son live in an old stone house in Jerusalem, within sight of the ancient city walls and the Valley of Gehenna. During the recent Yom Kippur War, he was commanding about twenty men not far away on the eastern edge of the city. Half his men were about ten years younger than he; the rest were teenagers. As wars go, it was a quiet one for Amichai, but it had its surreal moments, such as the time a prosperous-looking American came to his command post to ask if someone could translate the news broadcasts for him. He turned out to be Burt Lancaster. "There I was," says Amichai, "on the Mount of Olives translating war bulletins to an American who had come to Jerusalem to play Moses in a movie made by Italians."

One of the poems in *Songs of Jerusalem and Myself* is entitled "Suicide Attempts of Jerusalem." Does he mean to suggest, I wondered, that Jerusalem has a death wish? Amichai says, "It is such a tiny city so loaded with symbols. So many different religions seem dependent upon it. Sometimes I think people in the city wish it weren't so important, that it was a place just like Cincinnati."   (1974)

MAX APPLE

When Max Apple won a fellowship to Stanford University to study creative writing, his grandmother warned him not to go. Why, Apple wondered. You'll go blind, she said. All the scribes she knew back when she was a girl in Russia had bad eyesight and some of them even went blind. He explained that a writer was not the same as a scribe. Maybe she believed him, maybe she didn't, but she gave her grandson her blessing, and Max Apple, fresh from the University of Michigan, went west to California. That was thirteen years ago.

"For a writer," Apple says, "so much depends on who your grandmother is. Actually, Gorky said that, but I agree. My grandmother lived in the United States for over sixty years and she was consistently awed by the place, but what she loved most was telling stories about her old village. I'm sure she never thought of them as stories. She just talked away in Yiddish and, in time, she re-created the whole town for me. I've come to realize it's her voice that I hear as I write. She died in 1966, a year after my father."

It was his father's death that brought Apple back to Michigan. He gave up work on a sprawling realistic novel about the Russo-Japanese War and decided to become an academic. ("It seemed more financially responsible.") In due course he won his Ph.D. with a dissertation on Robert Burton's *The Anatomy of Melancholy* (1621) and now teaches at Rice University in Houston, Texas.

"Except," he says, "I didn't really give up. I kept my secret vice. I kept writing furtively to keep awake while I was doing the Ph.D. stuff. I look at my old notebooks. In the front are all my proper academic notes, and in the back there are strange little stories. They all begin realistically enough, and then fantasy drifts in. Castro pops up, or Howard Johnson, odd occurrences that didn't seem at all right for the kinds of stories I thought I should be writing."

A few of the stories appeared in small magazines and he sent one, "The Oranging of America," to Ted Solotaroff, editor of *The American Review*. *AR* published it, featured it on the front cover, and "Oranging"—a strange and funny tale of big business and cryonics (or of nature, man and God, if you prefer)—became the most talked-about short story of 1974. It was republished as the title story in a collection of ten Apple tales that should be read by anyone who is getting morose about the state of short fiction in America.

Like many short-story writers, Apple admits that he would really like to write a novel. "Unfortunately, after writing twenty-five pages I begin to panic," he says. He also gets literary competition from his 100-year-old grandfather, a retired baker. "When he heard I was getting paid for a book of short stories he was furious. 'I'm smarter than you are,' he said, and he started to work on a collection of Yiddish moral tales. So far, at least, he hasn't found a publisher." (1977)

MARGARET ATWOOD

Robertson Davies, the Canadian writer who won an international reputation with his novel *Fifth Business*, has observed a pecking order in literary criticism. "A Frenchman," he wrote in his collection of essays *A Voice from the Attic*, "can humiliate an Englishman just as readily as an Englishman can humiliate an American, and an American a Canadian. One of Canada's most serious literary needs is some lesser nation to domineer over and shame by displays of superior taste."

Well, Margaret Atwood, a young Canadian writer who has published three remarkable books in the last few months, has disregarded Mr. Davies' pecking order and has found a nation to shame with superior taste quite close at hand. It is in fact across the border and is called the United States. Canadians, she said during a recent visit to New York, are not yet culturally self-confident, but with 15 million English-language readers, Canadians buy more poetry per capita than any other nation on earth. "We import our junk," she adds, leaving little doubt about where she thinks Canadians import it from.

In the past year, Miss Atwood, who teaches English literature at the University of Toronto, has published a novel, *Surfacing*; a study of Canadian literature, *Survival*; and a book of poems, *Power Politics*. She had previously published one other novel and four collections of poetry.

Survival states a favorite theme of Miss Atwood's: that while the English are chiefly concerned with social classes and Americans with money, Canadians have been concerned with the basic experience of survival. "Canadians are forever taking the national pulse like doctors at a sickbed," she says. "The aim is not to see whether the patient will live well but simply whether he will live at all. Our central idea of survival is one which generates an almost intolerable anxiety."

Miss Atwood mirrors that sense of anxiety accurately in her poetry. The most frequently quoted poem from *Power Politics*, for instance, reads in its entirety:

> you fit into me
> like a hook into an eye
>
> a fish hook
> an open eye

Typical of the differences between the United States and Canada, as Miss Atwood sees them, is the way each treats its

Indians. Both countries have treated Indians shabbily, she thinks, but in Canada it was simply a matter of stupidity, in the United States the harm was done with malice. "But then," she adds, "Canadians tend to think they are much more righteous than the Americans." (1973)

BERYL BAINBRIDGE

In the past four years the young English novelist Beryl Bainbridge has published four books, and a fifth is due at her British publisher this fall. "They told me," she said during a visit to the United States, "that if I wasn't going to make a splash with one big book— and I wasn't—I should try to make it with a barrage of novels, one a year for five years." Her new novel, the fourth, is a fast-paced, ironic comedy called *Sweet William*, and it came out right on schedule.

This is her second career as a novelist. In the early 1960s she published two novels she prefers not to talk about. "They were flowery," she says. "Actually, I rather liked describing rooms and what people were eating, but an editor at Duckworth—they weren't the publishers of the fancy novels—told me that I wasn't writing correctly. He saw me as someone who should be writing sparse, spare novels. Duckworth, you know, was founded by Virginia Woolf's half brother, the one who treated her so illy when she was a girl. Later, he became her publisher, and D. H. Lawrence's too. He's dead now, of course."

Her first Duckworth novel was *Harriet Said*, and since

then she has maintained one of the most unusual publisher-author relationships I've heard of. She has a desk at Duckworth, which operates out of a 150-year-old former piano factory near the canal in the Camden Town section of London, and she does her rewriting there. "I do my first drafts at home, but they have me rewrite a lot. I spend twelve or thirteen weeks on each book. If I allowed myself more time I'd get lazy and not write a word." She also used to do odd jobs at Duckworth, and when *Harriet Said* came out, she was working there as a shipping clerk. "I suspect I'm one of the few novelists who ever packed up and mailed out their own books."

She says she doesn't write complete fiction. "Almost everyone in my books is based on someone real. I wrote *The Bottle Factory Outing* the year after I worked in a wine-bottling plant. I made up the part about the killing, of course, but I can tell you the real names of everyone in the book. They've all read it and don't seem to mind at all. Most people don't mind being in books, especially if you do something outlandish with them, like killing them off." Sweet William, the hero of her new novel, is also based on a real person, an appealing rogue who could literally charm the socks and a few bob off everyone he met.

Beryl Bainbridge's career has been a varied one. At the age of 5 she was tap dancing in Liverpool music halls. At 10 she entered a BBC school in Manchester and performed on children's radio programs. When she was 15 her mother took her to London and enrolled her in a ballet school. Later she joined a repertory theater company and appeared regularly on a television soap opera. At some point she also took up painting. "They were very primitive," she says. "I painted until I married a painter, and he was so much better that I gave up and started writing." She has three children.

She says she is surprised by how often she has been asked about women's liberation during her American visit. "In England, women's lib is more or less a hobby for middle-class divorcées. Here, every time someone interviews me I'm asked if I consider myself a woman writer. Well, I'm a woman and I

11.

write. Next question, please. I think the idea of liberation is balmy. Women have always been liberated. Nothing is equal. My mother's complaint was not that her life was unequal but that it was boring. Boring! I wonder, though, why there aren't more female writers in America. In England there are about nine female writers for every male. I suspect that over here, there are a lot of women who might have been writers but instead chose to go out and compete with men in business. I actually like to stay at home. You'll notice in *Sweet William* that it's the men who have the cars and bicycles. The women all stay at home."

Another thing that surprised her about America was New York City. "It seems so old, and I was expecting such a modern place. I swear it seems older than London. Nothing in England is old anymore. I went back to Liverpool not so long ago and I didn't recognize anything. Everything I remembered had been torn down and rebuilt. Sometimes I feel that I don't know anything about the present, and I don't care about the future. My past has been totally lost. My father used to use the expression, 'It's all me eye and Peggy Martin.' I have no idea what it means. I think it's something he picked up when he was a sailor. But it's things like that, things that don't really make sense anymore, that are all that I have left of the past. The novel that's due this fall is about my parents. It's the hardest thing I've ever written."   (1976)

BOBBY BAKER

Bobby Baker—the former Senate page who worked his way up to being Secretary of the Democratic Majority in the Senate, chief errand boy to Majority Leader Lyndon Johnson, owner of the Carousel Motel and inmate at the federal prison in Lewisburg, Pennsylvania—sat in a glossy midtown Manhattan restaurant and said, "The way to get ahead in the Senate is to find the senators' weaknesses and give them what they want." The pretty blond at his side nodded in agreement. Baker clearly followed the same formula when he, with the help of Larry L. King, wrote his autobiography, *Wheeling and Dealing.* "Of course it's full of scandal and corruption," he said. "That's what people want. The next one I write will be very professional and all about the good that men do, and it will be the sorriest thing you ever did see."

In 1942 Baker went from Pickens, South Carolina, to the United States Senate. He was 14. "I never had what you'd call a normal childhood. I grew up in the Senate, and if it hadn't been for that so-called scandal in 1963 I'd be senior man in the Senate today. I'd have outlasted them all," he says. What he doesn't say is that seniority doesn't mean much when you're not a senator. "Most people, and that includes most senators, are gutless cowards. They need leaders, and they want to follow. When you go to the circus they have performers and a ringmaster. Well, when I was in the Senate, I was ringmaster." All this is said in a soft Carolina drawl and with the sort of easy smile I suspect can only be learned by someone who was pouring bourbon and fetching cigars before he owned a razor.

A conversation with Baker, or at least the one I had, turns out to be a litany of near-slanderous snippets: what famous liberal senator is a "fraud"; who in the Senate "went down with everything but the *Titanic*"; what distinguished figure is a masochist (later Baker retracted that: he meant

13.

sadist); what well-known Southerner got so drunk and unruly one night that Baker broke "for the one time in my life" his golden rule of never providing professional prostitutes.

But here are some of his more printable remarks. On Truman: "When he left town he had only three friends, Bess, Margaret and Dean Acheson, but he was the kindest man I encountered in the Senate." On campaign contributions: "They're g.d. bribes." On Joe McCarthy: "When he came to Washington he was a breath of fresh air, but then he started drinking the whiskey. One night when he was drunk he read some speech a right-winger on his staff had written, all about Communists. For the first time in his life he got big headlines, and he never got over it. He kept on drinking and reading those speeches until it killed him." On Lyndon Johnson: "He had an excess of genius, and I had an excess of common sense. So we were a perfect team." On the Kennedys: "They just didn't have good manners, but if I had had my way I would have bred Lyndon with Bobby Kennedy, and Nixon would never have gotten close to the White House." On Nixon: "I told Bebe to burn those g.d. tapes, but there must be a Great Creator up there to have kept him from doing it." On Congress: "It's a comedy. The whole g.d. thing is show biz." On Bobby Baker: "One thing I know, I know who's buying who."

(1978)

DONALD BARTHELME

One of the standard author nightmares is the lost manuscript. Thomas Wolfe actually lost one in Germany in the 1930s. William Humphrey left the manuscript of *The Ordways* on an Italian train, but got it back. (As a result, the book is dedicated to the Italian National Railway.) After William Gass's only copy of *Omensetter's Luck* disappeared, he rewrote the whole novel from memory.

But Donald Barthelme—the short-story writer and novelist who just published a collection of parodies and other nonfiction entitled *Guilty Pleasures*—thinks that having to reconstruct a lost manuscript might not be such a bad idea after all. "It might even help the distillation process," he said the other day. Distillation is a word he uses frequently when he describes the way he writes: "I write a lot—every day, seven days a week—and I throw a lot away. Sometimes I think I write to throw away. It's a process of distillation."

"Eugénie Grandet," one of the parodies in *Guilty Pleasures*, is a masterpiece of distillation. In it, Barthelme reduces the Balzac novel to nine brisk pages. "It's an exercise in reduction," Barthelme says, "but it's not literary criticism. It's me saying, 'Look what I've done to your novel, Balzac. I made a toy out of it.'"

The book's title seems to suggest that Barthelme might regard the collection with some misgiving, a suggestion that is reinforced in his author's preface when he describes writing parodies as "a disreputable activity." But he says he has a clear conscience. "Parody is just a form of play, a kind of improvisational comedy. You start with a premise, hope it's funny and then let it rip." For his parody of Carlos Castaneda's *The Teachings of Don Juan: A Yaqui Way of Knowledge*, Barthelme said the premise that got him started was that the word Yaqui was not unlike Yankee. The result was "The Teachings of Don B.: A Yankee Way of Knowledge," which gets my vote as the funniest item in the book.

There are also two picture stories made up of old prints that Barthelme has cut up, re-pasted and set atop some curious captions. Sticking to his penitential phraseology, Barthelme calls these collages "a secret vice gone public." The vice is maintained by a huge collection of prints that he has picked up in his travels.

Barthelme has just completed his fifth collection of short stories (his stories tend to be very short: "I'm naturally short-winded," he says) and he is distilling away on his second novel, one that he has no intention of losing.   (1975)

GIORGIO BASSANI

Giorgio Bassani, one of Italy's most distinguished living novelists, is best known in this country through the film made from *The Garden of the Finzi-Continis*. Ironically, it is the only one of his five prose books that is out of print here. More ironic, as far as Bassani is concerned, is that none of his books of poetry has been published in English. He likes to call himself a lyric poet who also writes prose.

But Bassani's *The Smell of Hay* has just been published here, and that should dispel all talk of irony, at least for now. It is the last of five books set in Ferrara—Bassani's native city—which the author considers one long novel. *The Garden of the Finzi-Continis* is the centerpiece, and the new book, Bassani says, is "the consolidation of all my literary feelings." He adds, "I think of the Ferrara novels as a house, and the new book is the roof, a lyrical arabesque."

I myself suspect that the phrase "lyrical arabesque" sounds better in Italian than English. I think it sells the book short. It is a collection of short stories and a novella, all set in the late '30s and early '40s. The quality of the collection can best be suggested by the title. It refers to the city's Jewish cemetery. Inside the gate is a huge field that mowers keep cut. I'll quote from Bassani (as translated by Warren Weaver): "Once the hearse had passed the stone threshold of the broad gate—and in crossing it, the vehicle would jolt suddenly—a sharp smell, the smell of newly mown hay, would come to animate the procession, oppressed by the heat. What a relief. And what a peace."

Bassani has been visiting New York, and I mentioned the passage to him. He said, "Ah, yes, it's the sense of life against the death of a place." In Ferrara, he went on to say, which has one of the oldest Jewish quarters in Italy, there are almost no young Jews and very few older ones. "The young are all in Milan, and as for the elders, many either fled or were killed during the Nazi occupation."

The date of a story is very important to Bassani, and he is always careful to state it. In 1938 the Italian anti-Jewish laws were passed. In 1943 there were a few months of freedom and then the Germans arrived. Bassani, as a Jew and a member of the anti-Fascist underground, was imprisoned and after liberation went to Rome.

"The late '30s and early '40s," he says, "were the time of Italy's greatest crisis. You can't understand the country unless you understand what happened then. I'm a historical writer. I explain my country through a single city over a very few years."

I asked him about an oblique reference to Nathaniel Hawthorne in *The Gold-Rimmed Eyeglasses*, the novella in the new collection. "He's one of my favorite writers, my favorite American. We're quite similar, I think, in our concentration on a small part of our own countries. I also think we are both religious writers not involved in religion. My religion is the story of me and my country, a religion of the history of history."

Tennis plays an important role in many Bassani novels and stories. Does he play? "Oh, yes, very well. I was excellent when I was young. In '38 I won ten tournaments and was one of the best amateurs in the country, but then the anti-Jewish laws were passed and I could no longer play. The end of the war meant I could play again. Now, I write in the morning, and then, after lunch, I get nervous and have to play. Tennis is my sleeping pill." (1976)

ROMARE BEARDEN

In 1940 a young North Carolina–born artist named Romare Bearden rented studio space just down 125th Street from the famous Apollo Theater in Harlem and began his career. There have been a number of interruptions since then: the Army in World War II and after that a full-time job as a caseworker specializing in the gypsy community with the New York City Department of Social Services, which lasted, on and off, until the mid-1960s. But Bearden continued to paint, and he got to Paris, briefly, to study on the GI Bill. His style evolved from realism to abstract expressionism until, with a burst of creative energy in the '60s, he turned to assembling vivid collages.

A few years ago he had a major show at the Museum of Modern Art in New York, and this winter sees the publication of *The Art of Romare Bearden*, a lavish book focusing on his collages. Commenting on these vibrant mixtures of images from Harlem street life and ageless ritual, Bearden says, "I did the new book out of a response and need to redefine the image of man in terms of the black experience I knew best."

I recently visited Bearden (who looks like a trim Buddha in a blue knit sailor's cap) in his immaculate studio in the wholesale plastics district on Canal Street in Manhattan. He said his introduction to collage came by accident. Back in the early '60s he belonged to a group of artists who were trying their hands at various experiments (such as painting only in black and white), and someone suggested they try a communal painting, with many members of the group working on the same picture. The problem was how to start. Bearden cut some glossy pictures from his wife's fashion magazines with the idea that the pictures could be pasted on different backgrounds to form "sketches" for the final painting. On the day set aside for the communal effort no one showed up but Romare Bearden, so he started playing with the bits of paper himself. The result was his first collage.

Bearden is deeply concerned with what he calls "the prevalence of ritual," and a number of his collages deal with rituals, such as purification rites, that appear in different forms in radically different cultures. In one baptism collage, for instance, African masks are juxtaposed with steam engines (trains play a major role in his work: one critic sees them as symbols of the white man's intrusion upon the black world; Bearden says he sees them as artifacts of modern technology— which, of course, may be two ways of saying the same thing), hands from one photograph are glued onto arms from another, eyes from different faces are joined on a common head, city sidewalks and wooden fences blend into jungle.

I asked Bearden about his techniques of making collages. Does he keep files of photographs and bits of paper and cloth that he thinks might come in handy some day? He doesn't. Any photographs or magazine pictures, he says, will do. He begins by placing colored rectangles on larger sheets of paper and moving them about until a pattern suggests something. Then he tears up whatever pictures are handy (always tearing upward and then across on a right angle to destroy any sense of perspective that might intrude) and glues them solid. Later, he adds some paint.

"If you have enough confidence and patience things emerge. I never start with a preconceived idea of what I'll do. To do otherwise would be like a hunter setting out in the morning and saying he was going to shoot two deer, three pheasants and a rabbit. You have to take what you find. It's a feeling of adventure."   (1974)

ELIZABETH BISHOP

When the Modern Language Association, during its convention last December, began a long session devoted to Elizabeth Bishop and her poetry, Miss Bishop ducked out and went around the corner to a delicatessen. Why? "For one thing," she said the other day, "I don't know how anyone can sit through one of those meetings. For another, the Stage serves the best corned beef hash in Manhattan."

In 1969, when she won the National Book Award for her prematurely titled *The Complete Poems*, she was in Brazil (she lived there for sixteen years) and word was brought to her by the police. "I came back from shopping and outside my door were two men in uniform, one with a lot of gold braid and the other wearing a tin helmet. They both snapped to attention and saluted me. It scared my little maid to death."

This year she won the National Book Critics Circle Award for her new collection of poems, *Geography III*, and she came down to New York from Boston to accept the prize. For many of the critics at the ceremony it was their first chance to see one of the legendary figures of modern American poetry, a woman whose poems are as open and accessible as she is shy and reticent.

"I've gone up and down the East Coast," she said when we met recently, "living everywhere from Nova Scotia to Key West, but I've never seemed to live long enough in one place to become a member of a poetry 'group,' and when I was in Brazil there weren't any groups handy. I've been a friend of Marianne Moore's and Robert Lowell's but not a part of any school."

She seems amused by the fact that both Moore and Lowell became compulsive tinkerers who often reworked their poems even after they were published. "All that revision never interested me," she says, "but Marianne Moore's greatest influence on me was a thirst for accuracy. She would go to incredible pains to get things right." For "Crusoe in England," in *Geography III*, Miss Bishop had a friend visit a goat farm to find out how goats open their eyes, and for "The Moose" she searched through maps in the Boston and Harvard libraries in search of the name of a particular Nova Scotia swamp. She finally came across it in a secondhand-book store in Bermuda, in the yellowing memoirs of a 19th-century missionary. But she doesn't carry factual accuracy to pedantic extremes. "In the Waiting Room" describes a *National Geographic* magazine she read in a dentist's office in 1918, the February issue. "Out of curiosity I looked it up, and it turned out that I had combined the March and February issues, but I didn't change the poem. It was right the way it was. I think Robert Lowell thinks I carry the accuracy business too far. When he gave me his new manuscript to read, he said, 'Oh, you'll just find mistakes.'"

The poem that the judges of the National Book Critics Circle picked out for special mention was "The Moose," which mixes the events of a bus trip from Nova Scotia to Boston with memories of childhood. "It is one of the few poems my Canadian relatives have liked," she says. Although she was born in Massachusetts, she spent her early years with her grandparents in Nova Scotia. "It was written in bits and pieces over a number of years and, finally, it all came together.

After I read it in public for the first time, at Harvard, one of the students said, 'For a poem it wasn't bad.' "

One of the most moving poems in the book has for a refrain: "The art of losing isn't hard to master." It mentions three "loved houses." "Yes," she says, "one in Key West, one in Petrópolis, just west of Rio Bay, and one in Ouro Prêto, also in Brazil. The Ouro Prêto house was built in 1690, and from the front porch you can see seven baroque churches. I called it Casa Mariana, after Marianne Moore and because it was on the road to a town called Mariana. When I left I took the name plaque off the door. There are so many places I'll never go back to. I change, the places change. I was afraid to go back to Nova Scotia, but I went not long ago, and it hadn't changed."   (1977)

ISABEL BISHOP

Next to a corner window overlooking the trees and parking spaces of New York's Union Square, a trim, handsome 73-year-old grandmother wearing a paint-spattered hospital lab coat is taking trial impressions of an etching she has just made. She puts the etched plate and paper into a large handpress and adjusts the crank, which looks like a ship's wheel. Then she jumps up, grabs hold of one of the spokes of the wheel and rides it down to the floor. "That's the only way I can make the thing work," says Isabel Bishop.

Miss Bishop has been working next to that window for over forty years, painting or making etchings. Her subjects are usually taken from life in Union Square or from sketches she makes as she rides in on the subway from Riverdale each morning. This year the Whitney Museum staged a retrospective Bishop exhibition. Commenting on it in *The New York Times*, the art critic John Russell said, "This is someone who asked herself, 'What is it that is most important about human beings?' and came up with a set of very good answers." To mark the exhibition, the publishing firm of Harry N. Abrams, Inc., has issued *Isabel Bishop*, a lavishly illustrated volume with an interpretive essay by the art historian Karl Lunde.

Miss Bishop came to New York from Detroit in 1918 to study at the Art Students League. She says that she was fortunate in finding a teacher there who was "classical but not academic and who believed experiment was simply a fresh interpretation of tradition." She wanted to paint movement. "I wanted a sense of mobility—so a viewer could look at a picture and say, 'Turn your head,' and it would turn." Her teacher, though, did not believe in using live models, and it was only when she started sketching from life, she says, that "I got going on my own track."

She has used models ever since, but never professionals. In 1936 the Metropolitan Museum bought one of her paintings, a portrait of two waitresses from Childs restaurant on Union Square. After the recent Whitney show opened, Miss Bishop was surprised to receive a chatty letter from one of the waitresses, who now lives in California. She also used to use bums who loitered in the square as models ("The square is a shabby place, but it has *always* been shabby. It is one of the few parts of New York that hasn't changed"). She now prefers college students.

"I go up to Columbia or down to NYU and sketch them as they walk across the campus. Watch groups of students walk sometime. They are fascinating because they are sharing a temporary role. They are in transit. Even in groups, they come and go singly."

In recent years most Bishop paintings have been devoted to scenes of people walking, and amateur models come to her studio and pace back and forth as she sketches them. The walking paintings grew out of sketches done of the sprawling subway station under Union Square. The station is a confusing place, built on different levels, with gates and iron bridges and a ceiling composed of row after row of shallow arches. "I kept drawing the station," she says, "but every time I put people in, it looked as though they were in prison, which was all wrong. The essence of a subway station is that people aren't stable. They are just passing through. So I started studying those old Muybridge photographs of people walking. Then I moved on to doing my own fast sketches in the Muybridge style. This got me going on something entirely new: What do I see when I see people walking? It's a problem I'm still working on."

Another problem that interests her is the female nude. "People just aren't built the way they used to be. Women now have longer waists and no hips. I was painting a model not long ago and I posed her putting on panties. After a few minutes she said, 'No, this isn't valid,' and got dressed. She said, 'I'm not feminine, I'm sexy. I don't get dressed, I just put my clothes on.' That is an attitude I want to paint. Painting a nude is a terrific challenge—drawing them is actually quite simple—because a painting must be contemplatable."

Miss Bishop and Dr. Harold Wolff, a neurologist, were married in 1934, and it was from him that she got into the habit of wearing castoff lab coats while she worked in her studio. "They have big pockets, and they keep your clothes clean," she says. Dr. Wolff died in 1962 and most of his friends at Cornell Medical School, who used to pass on their coats to Miss Bishop, have retired. "I'm down to my last coat," says Miss Bishop, who has no intention of retiring. "I better take good care of it."   (1975)

Bob and Ray have been making people laugh since 1946, and that makes them the longest-running comedy team on radio or television. They have now published their first book. Called *Write if You Get Work*, the sign-off line they've used from the beginning, it is a collection of some of their best sketches, from the first episode of their soap opera *Mary Backstayge, Noble Wife* to a sample Bert and Harry commercial for Piel's Beer to an interview with Fentriss Synom, formerly a tree and furniture imitator, who now imitates food: franks and beans, a bottle of champagne, spaghetti and meatballs ("They want me to work on a chateaubriand, but I can't get the charcoal part right").

I dropped by radio station WOR the other afternoon to talk with them about the book and watch their three-hour daily broadcast. Bob is Bob Elliott, the smaller, sandier-colored one. He usually plays the straight-man role in their interviews and looks, as a Bob and Ray character might say, like a seasoned veteran of the sports desk on a large metropolitan newspaper. Ray is Ray Goulding, the larger, more florid one. He looks as though his picture might appear in the paper over the caption: Governor Names Brother to Head Racing Commission.

In 1946 Elliott and Goulding, staff announcers at a Boston station, were given the half-hour slot before Red Sox games to fill. They filled it with something called *Matinee with Bob and Ray*. "We had so much to do," Bob recalled, "that we didn't have time to write anything down. It was all ad lib, and most of our bits—some of which we are still doing—came out of what was going on at the station. Our announcer, Wally Ballou, was based on the station's janitor. Mary Backstayge was, of course, from *Mary Noble, Backstage Wife*. Our Mary has now been on the air longer than the original. We sometimes wonder if the kids out there know what we are parodying."

Ray adds, "We still ad lib *Mary*, although we now do it on tape because of all the characters and sound cues. One of the strangest things about getting ready for *The Two and Only*, the Broadway show we did a few years back, was going through our old tapes and memorizing what was never really written down."

When they broadcast, the two sit side by side at a snug horseshoe-shaped desk. The most surprising thing about their performance is that after thirty years on the job, they still take delight in the mechanics of broadcasting. They whistled or sang along with the commercials, commented on the quality of announcers' voices and joked about the station's "hard-hitting" editorial on a local strike, both of them shouting "however" a good half sentence before the editorial did. They laughed at the replays of the *Mary Backstayge* tapes and seemed to honestly enjoy the reactions they got from the engineer and director in the control room.

The program was a collage of straight news, weather and traffic reports, community announcements and Bob and Ray comedy bits. There was an interview with Mr. I Know Where They Are, who revealed the current whereabouts of the man who did the first live broadcast from Mammoth Cave and a movie starlet who made a name for herself in the Depression by dancing on a mink-covered stairway (she's assembling pocket calculators in New Jersey). There was an inaudible editorial rebuttal from a man who believed that talking too loud added to noise pollution and a lesson on how to use silverware: "12 percent of the population knows how to use a spoon, but only 4 percent knows how to use a knife and fork."

Dick Cavett came in during one of the news breaks. The three gleefully exchanged anecdotes about radio and television interviewers who have been physically attacked while on the air ("Then the guy reached across the microphone and caught him square on the chin"), and I was reminded of one television critic who claimed Bob and Ray's humor "raises welts."

That's really not true. Bob calls their parodies satire, but there really isn't much moral outrage in their comedy. Kurt Vonnegut, in the foreword he has written for *Write if You Get Work*, comes closer when he writes: "Man is not evil, they seem to say. He's simply too hilariously stupid to survive." But that's not quite right either. Anyone who has heard them chuckle over an announcer for *Mid-Week Prayer* unctuously thanking a well-worn recording of "Bless This House" suspects that even if we are hilariously stupid, Bob and Ray, at least, are enjoying every moment of it.   (1976)

HEINRICH BÖLL

Heinrich Böll, the West German who won the 1972 Nobel Prize for Literature, was in town a few weeks ago and observed that Germans who have left Germany seem more "German" than the ones who remained at home. "Germany has changed a lot since the war," Böll says, "and the emigrant Germans have missed those changes." As a result many emigrants have become the repository of the old Prussian stereotypes now rarely encountered in Germany itself.

Since both Böll and Leila Vennewitz, his English-born translator, were here, I talked to them about how they go about translating a Böll novel. Mrs. Vennewitz's immediate answer was direct enough: "Start at the beginning and go straight to the end." Then she added, "I can't overestimate the value of Heinrich Böll's help. His grasp of English is excellent."

Considering that Böll lives in Cologne and Mrs. Vennewitz in Vancouver, British Columbia, the two have worked remarkably closely for ten years. They meet in person at least once a year, Mrs. Vennewitz says, and between meetings correspond about translation problems. One small point may take three or four letters to work out. A typical problem was the section in *Group Portrait with Lady* dealing with the making of funeral wreaths. Mrs. Vennewitz simply did not understand what the technical words in German meant. So she wrote to Böll. Böll replied that he himself had had no idea of how to make wreaths but read up on it in a training manual. He then Xeroxed the manual and mailed it off to Vancouver, where Mrs. Vennewitz took it to a local florist and with his help worked out the translation.

Böll, whose wife, Anne-Marie, is the German translator for a number of American novelists, is more deeply involved in the craft of translation than most authors. When Mrs. Böll finishes a translation, she reads it aloud and her husband follows along in the English-language edition. Mrs. Vennewitz, incidentally, uses a similar method: she reads aloud her English translation, while her husband, who is half German, follows along in German. Böll finds this involvement with translation useful: "It forces me deeper into the meaning of my own language."   (1973)

GEORGE BOOTH

A few days after George Booth and I met to talk about his new cartoon collection, *Rehearsal's Off!*, he called up to say that there was something very important that he had forgotten to tell me. "I always listen to country and western music while I draw," he said. "That's something cartoonists always ask each other: What do you listen to while you work? Be sure to put that in because I want to say something in the interview that might interest other cartoonists."

Booth, who looks something like a jovial Solzhenitsyn and talks with a slow Missouri drawl, listens to his favorite singers—Johnny Cash, David Allan Coe and Mel Tillis, whom he especially likes because Tillis sometimes stutters—late at night when, he says, "things are peaceful." Then he draws his comic world of sulking cats, nervous dogs and fractious amateur musical societies. "Sometimes I sit there and see nothing funny at all and then my belly draws up and I'll laugh and laugh. Being funny is hard work, but you get a lot of fun out of it, too."

Booth lives with his wife and daughter on the North Shore of Long Island. They share their house with two cats, Savortooth and Jerbones, who make frequent appearances in Booth's drawings. "I also have an imaginary dog in my head, an English pit bull terrior, and I draw him, too. He's very friendly, if you stay on the right side of him." Since 1970 Booth's cartoons have been appearing regularly in *The New Yorker*, and last year his first collection, *Think Good Thoughts About a Pussy Cat*, was a big seller during the Christmas season. His first published cartoons appeared in *Leatherneck* magazine just after World War II. Booth was then a marine, but he says he always wanted to be a cartoonist. He can remember as a young boy staying up as late as 2 A.M. drawing pictures with his mother. "That's when I began to be a night person," he says.

He thinks it important for a cartoonist to write his own captions. "I didn't use to think of myself as a writer as well as an artist, but now I do. I shy away from using other people's gags, because the creation of the caption is as much a part of the cartoon as the drawing. All cartoons don't have to have captions, but it is not a complete cartoon when you just illustrate a joke. When I first started drawing for *The New Yorker*, they'd sometimes give my captions to one of the house writers, Peter De Vries or someone else, to fix up. Now I spend almost as much time writing and rewriting as drawing.

"I don't analyze something and then do a cartoon about it. The analysis, when it comes at all, comes later. Funny words, or at least words I think are funny, often get me going in the direction of a gag. The other day I read somewhere that one of John Adams' political opponents was named Pinckney. Pinckney, that's a funny name, and I've just put it into a cartoon. There's a rock drummer named Zoob. That's a name I could do something with. Outside Keokuk, Iowa, which is along the Mississippi River, there's something called the Keoississippi Shopping Center. That's funny; so are words like *placate, worm, curmudgeon.*

"I've owned four Model A Fords since I came to New York, and maybe I've found a gag or two there. I once bought an old three-wheeled wicker beach chair thinking I might get a cartoon out of it, and I did. But then we have a rooster that crows every morning, and I have yet to get a gag out of that.

"I get annoyed by cartoonists who try too hard to be timely. They get their ideas from *The New York Times*, and it shows. The source should never show. The newspapers I give a real going over are small-town papers written by amateurs.

"I agree with E. B. White when he says that analyzing humor is like dissecting a frog. You can spread the pieces all over the table, but in the process you lose something. The important thing for me is to see the little things that everyone sees, the things they see and ignore, things that are so familiar you don't notice them, and laugh at them until they are drawn on paper." (1977)

ANDRÉ BRINK

André Brink, a South African novelist, has presented his government with what he hopes will be "an interesting tactical problem." His new novel, *Rumours of Rain*, is just about to be published in South Africa. It contains extensive quotations from Bram Fischer, an antiapartheid figure who is officially banned. That is, nothing he has said or written is allowed to be printed within the country. Brink, however, puts Fischer's words into the mouth of a fictional character on trial for fomenting black revolution, and each of the statements is rebutted by the novel's narrator, an Afrikaner businessman who is definitely not antiapartheid.

"I can't wait to see how they handle this one," Brink said during a recent visit to the United States. The South African Supreme Court "handled" his first novel, *Looking for Darkness* (1976), by banning it for being "pornographic, blasphemous and communistic."

Brink teaches modern Afrikaans literature at Rhodes University in Grahamstown and finds the government attitude toward him unpredictable. "They open my mail before I receive it. Sometimes they make it very obvious that I'm being followed, and once they confiscated my typewriter for a few months. When I returned home after my last foreign trip, they called me in and showed me a list of the names of all the people I had met abroad. They didn't do anything, or say anything; they just showed me the list to keep me on my toes."

Rumours of Rain is a long, beautifully crafted novel that uses the days leading up to the Soweto riots as a framework to tell the story of a successful Afrikaner businessman, his sturdy farmer parents, his son, who is a bitter veteran of the Angola War, his rebelliously liberal mistress and his former best friend—on trial for his life—whom he has betrayed.

Brink, who comes from an old Boer family, was not exposed to English until he was 14. "Then," he recalls, "my mother established 'English Day,' one day a week when we got punished if we spoke Afrikaans." He writes the first drafts of his novels in Afrikaans, and then does a new draft—not a translation—in English. "In the end," he says, "I have two different books. Afrikaans is like French in that you can get away with being terribly sentimental, something you can't get away with in English."

Afrikaners may be sentimental but, unlike Americans, Canadians or Australians, they rarely seem to have enjoyed any sense of triumph or satisfaction in their taming of the wilderness. "The Afrikaner," Brink says, "feels that he must always explain and defend his actions to the outside world—and to himself. He is at his best when he is suffering or oppressed. When he is in power, he is at his worst. He knows he is outnumbered by the blacks, and he knows there is always the time factor. He is reminded of it even when he watches a TV show like *Kojak*, where there are even black and white crooks who are equal. The clock is running, and Afrikaners, all of us, know we cannot stop it." (1979)

JAMES M. CAIN

James M. Cain, who was born in 1892, published his first novel when he was 42 years old—after a successful career as a newspaper reporter and an unsuccessful one as a film writer. This was *The Postman Always Rings Twice*. Later came such books as *Mildred Pierce* and *Double Indemnity*, and now, at 82, he is publishing his seventeenth, *Rainbow's End*. Another novel, already written, will be coming out next year, and there are at least two more in the works.

Cain still puts in a four-hour writing day (usually producing about 1500 words) in his white frame house just over the Maryland state line from Washington, D.C. He writes in longhand on legal-size yellow tablets while lying on a couch in his living room. The walls of the room are hung with framed programs and reviews tracing the operatic career of the singer Florence Macbeth, one of Cain's late wives (there have been four wives in all). The only mementos of his own career are two front pages from *Lorraine Cross*, the 79th Division newspaper, which he edited during World War I, and a ceramic bust of Poe, the Mystery Writers of America's "Edgar" award, which Cain won in 1970 in recognition of his writing career as a whole. "What they didn't seem to know," Cain says, "is that I wrote only one mystery story in my life and I made a mess of it."

Looking back over that long career, Cain seems particularly interested in talking about novels that didn't quite work out—such as an unpublished one written before *Postman* that dealt with West Virginia coal miners—and about the men he worked with on the *Baltimore Sun* and the *New York World*, notably H. L. Mencken and Walter Lippmann, "two Christ-awful reporters who were good on commentary but couldn't write a straight news story that would tell you anything."

Mildred Pierce is probably his best-known novel. Cain says that it is not one he remembers with satisfaction. A movie producer once said to him, "All characters in B pictures act too smart." That, he thinks, was his mistake with Mildred. He made her too smart, and as a result she struck people as being heroic. "She wasn't heroic," he says, "she was just plain common." Another producer once told him, "What I like about your books is that they are about dumb people who get into interesting situations," and that, Cain says, is the formula he likes best.

When he was working on the unpublished coal-mining novel, Cain recalls, he talked to Mencken about the troubles he was having with it. Mencken just humphed and said, "Three years in a man's life, that's a novel." To which Cain says, "If there was ever a hopeless comment by a man who had no idea of how to write a novel, that's it."

Though often regarded as a California writer, Cain has actually spent only a minor portion of his life there, only about seventeen years. He was born in Maryland, the son of the president of Washington College, and worked in Baltimore and New York City until some dialogue pieces he wrote for Mencken's *American Mercury* caught the eye of someone in Hollywood. Cain thinks that the greatest mistake he ever made was coming back East after the Hollywood years, for in the move, he feels, he lost his sense of acclimation with a useful geographic area. "No matter how you small it down," he says, "people want to read about Southern California. Who the hell cares about Prince Georges County, Maryland?" His new novel, *Rainbow's End*, is again set in coal-mining country.

The novel Cain is currently writing, *The Cocktail Waitress*, touches on a Maryland political scandal. "I take politics seriously," he says, "but I can't get interested in the small intrigues that get politicians their jobs." And that, of course, led us to Watergate. "I kept waiting for the Watergate Roxy Stinson to surface," he said.

It seems that Roxy's testimony proved to be a turning point during the Senate hearings that followed the Teapot Dome scandals of the Harding administration. Roxy was the divorced wife of one of the principals (who had, incidentally, committed suicide); she knew where the bodies were buried; and she told all.

"Her testimony ran for days in *The New York Times* and it was a literary sensation. She spoke in nothing but clichés, but she made them work. Take a look at Hemingway's short story 'Fifty Grand' sometime. There are paragraphs in there which directly reproduce Roxy's style."

And how about James M. Cain, I asked, did Roxy have any effect on him? "I hadn't begun *Postman* at that time, and she taught me respect for the cliché. I'd say she influenced me plenty."

He continued, "If you have any sense you write the kind of novel other people write, but the trick is you can't write the sort of novel anyone else has already written."   (1975)

HENRI CARTIER-BRESSON

My favorite dining-out story used to be about the time in 1959 when I was hitchhiking in France and got a ride with Henri Cartier-Bresson. I didn't know who he was but there were two Leicas on the front seat of his car and for a couple of hours we talked about photography and photographers. The punch line of the story—which can be dragged out interminably—comes when he says that I've mentioned only American photographers and wonders if there are any Europeans I admired. Then I say there's only one: Henri Cartier-hyphen-something.

Since then I've become aware of the mystery that surrounds Henri Cartier-Bresson. His name appears high on just about everyone's list of great photographers. He was the first photographer to be exhibited in a one-man show at the Louvre (1954); he introduced the phrase "the decisive moment" to describe the image a photographer seeks; since before the Spanish Civil War his pictures have appeared in magazines, books and museums throughout the world. Yet, there are almost no photographs of him in print (the one usually used for publicity purposes has been around for years and in it his face is partially hidden); he rarely gives interviews; and he is usually described by those who have seen him at work as being all but invisible.

Cartier-Bresson recently made one of his rare visits to New York from his home in Paris, and I was able to meet him once again. He was in town to attend the opening of the new International Center of Photography, which features a showing of pictures he took in Russia in 1954 and in 1972–73. The newer photographs have been published as a handsome book entitled *About Russia*.

At 67, Cartier-Bresson is precise in speech and dress. He has been bothered by arthritis in his right hand, but he says this has not affected his use of the camera. Wherever he goes he carries his Leica cradled on his arm: to wear it around his neck or over his shoulder would slow him down if he saw a picture to take. He is polite, even courtly, but he does not want to be quoted on anything that might be thought political. The same aversion to editorial comment can be seen in his pictures. "I have no overall view I want to present," he says. "I want people to look at the photographs and find what's there for themselves."

He does, though, want to dispel the notion that he is a photojournalist. "Journalism has kept me from going stale, and through photo assignments I am able to see many new places, but I am not a journalist. I simply sniff around and take the temperature of a place. I'm not interested in photographs that are 'made,' situations that are set up. I'm interested in discovering what is there. It is a recognition, like a shout. The secret is in concentration, in intuition. You must not think or try to prove or illustrate anything."

Photography, he says, *doesn't* prove anything. A camera does not document but raises questions, and a picture is only the evocation of a place or a situation. "Actually, I'm not all that interested in the subject of photography," he says. "Once the picture is in the box, I'm not all that interested in what happens next. Hunters, after all, usually aren't cooks. The joy is in seeing."

Although he avoids political questions, Cartier-Bresson is

especially upset by the amount of waste he sees in the world ("The ecologists are the only ones who speak to the future"), and photographers are as spendthrift as everyone else: "They should use less film and simply wait for pictures. Shooting too much is a sign of immaturity, and anyway you get better results if you shoot less. Time is the only luxury—use it. Being in a hurry is painful to me. A photographer must spend most of his time saying no. I say no, so I can say yes. I watch and say no, no, no, no, no and finally yes. Then I have it, a picture."

He finds the new romanticism that has attached itself to photography repulsive (much of this he blames on the popularity of the film *Blow-Up*), but he admits: "There's some magic in it. We pick pockets. We steal an image. There is joy in waiting to catch the moment. *Pfff*," his eyes widen and he snaps a picture with his fingers, "it's an affirmation." (1975)

JOHN CHEEVER

John Cheever: 62 years old, five-feet-six or so, with neatly trimmed 1950s hair, crewneck sweater, chinos and loafers. One glance, and you suspect you know just about how he looked nearly forty-five years ago when he was expelled from Thayer Academy. What you see, properly rumpled with the usual accumulation of lines, is an almost archetypal New England prep school face.

One story says he was thrown out of Thayer for smoking; another (Cheever's own) says he was a "lousy student." Whatever the reason, he never went back to school again, but promptly sold his first short story—"Expelled"—to *The New Republic*. Eventually he made his way to New York City, where he paid the rent on a boardinghouse room on Hudson Street by turning out scenarios for MGM, at five dollars each. Since then he has made his living as a writer: 250 stories (by his count), most of which appeared first in *The New Yorker*, and three novels, including *The Wapshot Chronicle*, winner of a 1958 National Book Award. *The World of Apples*, his sixth collection of short stories, has just been published.

I drove up to Ossining to talk with John Cheever in his handsome 18th-century Dutch stone farmhouse. Set deep into the side of a hill facing away from the Hudson River (and Sing Sing Prison, for that matter), the old Boatman place is the home of Cheever, his wife, Mary, their youngest son, Fredrico, a dowager Labrador retriever named Flora and several cats. The property includes a brook (newly polluted by some mysterious source upstream), several ponds and an apple orchard through which Cheever enjoyed skiing until a recent accident stopped him.

Cheever maintains a rather studied indifference toward *The World of Apples*. He says he never rereads a story once it is written, and his best stories, he adds, are written in three-day spurts and then forgotten. But the book seems to me to be a mellow collection, more mellow than usual for Cheever. Many of the stories deal with people whose lives have come to a moment of pause, giving them time to look back. True, there are the hints of madness and mystery which always lie just under the surface of a Cheever story: the husband who suddenly stuffs a kitten into the blender; the unknown authors who write romantic, Victorian novels on men's room walls, where once they wrote obscene words. All in all, it must be one of the most humane books of the season.

Why has John Cheever stayed with the short story and why do his novels often read like short-story cycles? He says, "All my relationships have been interrupted. I never know where my characters come from or where they are going. The short-story form proved very accommodating." He paused for a more apt word than "accommodating," but let it go.

38.

It is when talking about his early days as a *New Yorker* writer (he can give an excellent imitation of Ernest Hemingway emptying the Rose Room of the Algonquin Hotel with a string of profanity) or his two trips to Russia that Cheever becomes most animated. His novel *Bullet Park* sold better in Russia than in the United States.

"Literature," he says, "is the most acute and intimate form of communication we have, and perhaps because the Russians have fewer distractions—little or no television, for instance—they can appreciate that more than we do."

What Cheever seems to enjoy most about Russia is his friendship with the poet Yevgeny Yevtushenko, who turned to him one day in a crowded Moscow elevator and in a burst of emotion said, "You have a perfect working-class face."

Then Cheever turned to the fact that he is over 60. "There is so much I've had to give up. I get cross with dogs. I'm a man who talks to dogs." He is currently at work on a novel, a long novel, the longest thing he has ever written. And when he finishes, he says, he will stop writing. Then he adds that maybe he will write but he won't publish anything. He squints his old schoolboy eyes and looks as though he didn't believe a word of it.   (1973)

ELEANOR CLARK

It has been twenty-five years since Eleanor Clark published *Rome and a Villa*, and now, in honor of the new Holy Year, the book is being reissued with some updating and a few new chapters. To prepare the revised edition she revisited Rome and is sad to report that had she been seeing Hadrian's Villa for the first time she probably never would have been inspired to write about it.

She remembers her first visit, in the late 1940s, as a "mesmerizing experience." She and some friends had a picnic in the ruins, and the afternoon remains, she says, "as one of the most vivid memories of my life." She continues, "We took a Roman nap in the grass after lunch, and there was no sound but the buzzing of bees. I don't want to sound like a visionary sap, but I entered into the spirit of the place. Now that's all lost. The villa's crowded with tourists and buses. If there were any bees there now it would be impossible to hear them."

It seems typical of Miss Clark that a book was inspired by a place. She and her husband, Robert Penn Warren, live in what might be called semirural Connecticut, a setting not unlike that of her novel *Baldur's Gate*. Their home is a restored 18th-century barn. When they bought the building in 1953, she says, "there were cows downstairs, hay upstairs." She began writing *Rome and a Villa* while living in a ruined 16th-century fortress north of Rome. At first, she says, she didn't know she was writing a book at all, but simply making notes about aspects of Rome and the Emperor Hadrian. After she and Warren married and had their first child, Rosanna, they continued to vacation there. Warren wrote a poem about it for their daughter—"To a Little Girl, One Year Old, in a Ruined Fortress." It begins:

> To a place of ruined stone we brought you,
>   and sea-reaches.
> *Rocca:* fortress, hawk-heel, lion-paw,
>   clamped on a hill.
> A hill, no. On a sea cliff. . . .

Last year Rosanna, now a student at Yale, revisited the fortress. It was locked up tight, but obviously the new owners—the Pontis, Carlo and his wife, Sophia Loren—had spent a lot of money fixing the place up. Rosanna, her mother said, had to content herself with a peek through the keyhole in the gate and a picnic in the dry moat.

A summer the Warrens spent in Brittany resulted in Eleanor Clark's fascination with the oyster business (again she thought she was just taking notes) and a book, *The Oysters of Locmariaquer*, which won a National Book Award in 1964. A novella, *Dr. Heart* (which has just been published in a collection with a dozen of her earlier stories), grew out of a year spent in Grenoble. The Warrens, by chance, rented a house on Stendhal's father's farm, a place Stendhal wrote a good deal about. "You could feel him there," she says. "It became obsessive."

She converted a toolshed into a study and began the novella, which turned out to be about an American graduate student in Grenoble who becomes fascinated with both Stendhal and the *nouveau roman*. "I'm afraid I'll be *persona non grata* if anyone in Grenoble ever hears about the book, but it really is a forbidding, unfriendly city."

She admits, though, that if they had spent that year in Paris there probably would have been no book. "I can't function under so-called intellectually stimulating surroundings, and I can't stand faddish intellectual 'fashions.' *Dr. Heart* grew out of my feelings for an old house rather than dry discussion. I never begin a story with an *idea*. In fact, I like to quote the Yeats line, 'Ideas rob a man of his imagination.' I have to be smitten by a subject—and then it's total immersion or nothing. Writing, at least for me, is a delightfully mysterious business. I poke around and wait for something to explode in my head."

Miss Clark calls these moments "lucky accidents" and lately has found that they are inspired more often by her listening to music than by her reading. "We are all being battered by too much violence. A good deal of contemporary fiction is strained by an effort to match this violence. The idea used to be for a writer to learn the craft of writing. Now, it is too often a search for a vehicle to support a sense of violence. There's a fetishism about being of one's own time. That might be all well and good, but one shouldn't be undone by one's own time."

Before I interviewed Miss Clark in Connecticut I had been warned that a subject I should avoid was the rather obvious fact that both she and her husband were writers. Naturally, before I left, I had to ask her about that. Her answer was a hearty laugh. "We are different kinds of writers. As for the fact that he's won all these prizes, I think that's just dandy. I'm very proud of him, and I think he's very proud of me. As for fighting for status, we just don't do that."

Each of them has a study in one of the farm's outbuildings, and at their Vermont ski house each has a separate writing cabin in the woods. ("We write in the summer and ski in the winter.") Every day they write until 2 P.M., when they have lunch together.

As I was leaving the house I met Mr. Warren in the former barnyard. He was wearing high rubber boots and was returning from tinkering with the tractor. I said that Miss Clark had said she thought he was proud of her. "Sure I am," he said, "that's not at all hard to be." (1975)

MALCOLM COWLEY

"**I**t's as though I were a cop killer," Malcolm Cowley said the other day. "They sent me up for life with no chance for parole." Cowley, who will be 80 in August, was talking about his sixty years as a professional writer. It all began when Cowley, then a Harvard dropout, settled in Greenwich Village with his girlfriend, Peggy. An old friend of Peggy's was an editor on *The Dial*, and he let Malcolm review novels at a dollar a throw. "I'd pick up a pile of books at the magazine and go over to Union Square, where I could polish off six in an afternoon and then sell them at a secondhand-book store on Fourth Avenue for thirty-five cents a copy. The dollar a review came only on publication. The thirty-five cents was cash on the barrelhead, and that's what kept us in groceries and coal." Later would come the publication of Cowley's own books of poetry, history and literary criticism, his French translations, his editorship at *The New Republic* and his friendships with the likes of Hart Crane, Hemingway, Fitzgerald, Wolfe, Stein and Faulkner on to John Cheever (whose first short story he published) and Ken Kesey (who was his student at Stanford).

To celebrate his sixtieth anniversary as a writer, Cowley has just completed—*And I Worked at the Writer's Trade,* which combines informal autobiography with some serious thought about the vagaries of literary fame. "I now see myself as a literary historian," Cowley said when we talked about his new book, "and I'm especially interested in the waves of new literary generations. They come about every fifteen years and reflect a complete change in style and judgment, but the waves alternate between expansion and contraction, from looking outward to looking inward. I think I've lived through six ages so far." Beginning at the turn of the century, they are the Reform or Muckraking Age (outward looking), the Lost Generation (inward looking), the Jazz Age (outward) followed by the Depression, which Cowley believes lasted until 1945 and is something of an anomaly. After the war came the Silent Generation (inward), then the Rebellious Generation (outward), and we are now in the Me Generation (inward), which is marked by literature Cowley finds "unpeopled and inhuman."

Through all these alternating generations literary reputations are made and broken. "I never cease to be amazed why some of my friends became famous and others, just as talented, didn't. I've come to suspect it's a matter of wanting fame or not, and those who don't want it, don't get it." But fame can be fleeting. "I doubt if Thomas Wolfe will ever be popular again. By always saying in ten words what he could say in three, he put a terrible burden on future readers, while Hemingway would never say in three words what he could say in two. His reputation will be in eclipse for awhile but he'll be back. When I read a good Hemingway short story I can smell pine needles, and I can't say that about anyone else."

—*And I Worked at the Writer's Trade* ends with an intriguing sentence: "No complete son of a bitch ever wrote a good sentence." Cowley says, "The key word there is 'complete.' You can point to a lot of S.O.B.s (Hemingway, perhaps), but few complete ones. No writer has total control over his images and rhythm, so if a person is completely false, it will come out somehow in what he writes, and you can see it on the page."

I asked Cowley why he had never written fiction. "My essay style is really very close to fiction. You can easily read *Exile's Return* as a novel. But I'm not good at observing character. I suspect that so much of my life has been spent reading that I haven't looked around enough." With that, Malcolm Cowley headed back to Connecticut, where he is at work on his next book, his memoirs of the 1930s.   (1978)

ELIZABETH CULLINAN

The phrase "Irish Catholic" pops up in just about every short story in Elizabeth Cullinan's impressive new collection, *Yellow Roses*. A character, usually a girl in her late 20s, will have to describe herself and that's the phrase she uses, Irish Catholic. That's also the phrase Elizabeth Cullinan uses to describe herself.

"It's terrible, isn't it?" she said recently. "Irish Catholic sounds so parochial. I hate to see it in reviews of my books, and it's always there, usually in the first paragraph. But it's true. My parents are American, but all my grandparents were born in Ireland. I never went to a school that wasn't run by nuns. My family, my mother's family in particular, is full of nuns and priests. I never knew a Protestant to speak of until I got a job as a typist at *The New Yorker*. Some writers get beyond themselves and write about worlds they've never known, but I can't. I don't want to, and I suppose even if I did want to, I couldn't."

Soon after she graduated from Marymount Manhattan College in the late 1950s, she went to *The New Yorker* ("I was the only typist who knew how to take dictation, so I got to talk with everyone") and later became the secretary of fiction editor William Maxwell.

"I typed his novel, *The Chateau*, three or four times and that's really where I learned everything I came to know about writing. It was freaky, then, for a secretary to get anything published in the magazine. I'm really not sure why I started writing. It might have been simply because all my friends were getting married and there was no one I wanted to marry. So I wrote instead and *The New Yorker* took what I wrote.

"It was a funny thing. The makeup department was then almost 100 percent Irish Catholic, and the men there would tease me about whether I'd been to Mass or whether I was going to march in the St. Patrick's Day parade."

To write her novel, *House of Gold*, which deals with an Irish-American family, she went to Dublin and stayed there for three years. "Oddly enough," she says, "my family had no ties at all in Ireland, and they were mystified by my wanting to live there. When I came back with a tremendous Irish accent, that mystified them even more. The Irish in Ireland, you know, are really very different from the American Irish and don't look too kindly on their American cousins. They just can't take all that sentimentality too many Irish-Americans have toward old Mother Ireland. But I loved Dublin and I loved all that rain. I think I came back a different person. I became wary of saying silly things. Say something silly there and they'll shout you down."

In 1971, a year after the novel was published, she brought out her first collection of short stories, *The Time of Adam*, and is now at work on a new novel. It's set in Ireland and she is writing it on the East Side of Manhattan. "I really don't understand why people don't read more short stories, all those commuters going back and forth with time on their hands. A nice short-story book would be perfect for them. Luckily, *The New Yorker* pays very well, so I write short stories, even though I'm a shockingly slow writer, to have the luxury of writing novels. In a short story you're always writing toward an ending; you're always closing a short story off. With a novel you're right in the water and you swim with it."

As our interview came to an end, Elizabeth Cullinan said, "Let me ask you something. Do you think I'm insanely polite? John Leonard called me that in *The New York Times*. I think he's probably right, but I used to be more so. Now I can put my elbows on the table and just leave them there because it's more comfortable that way. I do think, though, that manners are a great help in getting one through the day. They just make everything so much easier." (1977)

PETER DE VRIES

Peter De Vries, who over the past thirty-six years has written some of the funniest novels published in the United States, said recently that he wondered "why people seem to want permission to laugh." Critics, he says, delight in pointing out the darker shadows in his novels, as if to justify the humor. "Ministers keep asking me to give sermons on the crises of our times. Maybe it's because everything is going to hell in a handbasket, just as I've been saying for years."

Princeton Theological Seminary once offered him its annual L. P. Stone Lectureship. The lectureship was established in 1883 to "provide a lecturer, chosen by the faculty, to speak on a topic related to theological studies." De Vries says, "I assumed it was a clerical error and declined."

"Everyone seems to have a theory about humor. Analysts talk about what we laugh at, but not why we laugh. I don't think you can separate laughter from grief. It's like talking about H_2O and not talking about H or O. Faulkner was our greatest comedian. No one has been funnier, and no one has been more bitter than Thurber or Twain. Talking about theories of comedy is like a woman squeezing into a girdle that's too small. There are so many things to laugh at, nothing fits. There's always an overflow."

De Vries claims to be especially fond of mimicry and impersonation. "It's a bewitching art, and it isn't simply the joy of seeing genius deflated. The parodies you most enjoy are of people you like the most." His new novel, *I Hear America Swinging*, a jaunty yarn dealing with what happens when the greening of America hits the tall corn of Iowa, begins with a parody of Walt Whitman: "I hear America swinging, / The carpenter with his wife or the mason's wife, or even the mason, / The mason's daughter in love with the boy next door, who is in love with the boy next door to him, / Everyone free, comrades in arms together, freely swinging. . . ."

I asked which came first, the novel or the parody. "I can't ever remember the original idea for a novel once it's finished," he said. "I think it is like blotting out the pain of childbirth." What really came first, dating back more than a decade, was the debut of Clem Clammidge, the novel's "primitive art critic," formerly a hired man. Clem made his first appearance—wearing a plaid hunting jacket and a cap with earflaps—in a brief item De Vries planted in a column in the *Saturday Review*. It told of this strange bumpkin who was causing quite a flap in local New England art galleries by turning up at openings and making homespun comments on what he saw.

"I thought it was time for a primitive critic," De Vries recalls. "It seems that the simpler the artistic endeavor—say, pop art—the more arcane the criticism of it seems to become. I was just trying to cut things back to size."

With seventeen books to his credit, De Vries looks fit and hardy, although he says he has to watch what he does and what he eats because of a mild heart condition ("Fibrillation rhymes with tribulation") and an inflammation called thrush in his throat ("Thrush is no lark even though it makes you swallow"). He commutes to his office at *The New Yorker*, where he has worked since 1944, from his home in Connecticut.

"There are some critics who keep telling me that I should cut out the jokes and get serious, *really* serious. Granville Hicks on the old *Saturday Review* would almost have a heart attack each time one of my new books came out. 'No more jokes. No more jokes,' he'd say, and I'd solemnly vow never to write another joke. Then I'd sit down and write the first sentence of the next novel and I'd be in trouble. Take *I Hear America Swinging*. I sat down and the first thing I knew I'd written: 'I had just been through hell and must have looked like death warmed over walking into the saloon, because when I asked the bartender whether they served zombies he said, "Sure, what'll you have?" ' and I was off again. It's like an alcoholic's first drink." (1976)

JAMES DICKEY

"**A**s a Southern Baptist," James Dickey was saying, "I feel that I was born at the tail end of decadent Puritanism." He was in New York City promoting his new book-length poem, *The Zodiac*, and at 10 A.M. he had just returned to his hotel room after doing a bit of grocery shopping. A brown shopping bag full of half-quart cans of Colt 45 malt liquor leaned against the dressing-table mirror. A Texas-style safari hat and a sheepskin jacket were piled on a chair. He wore an Irish fisherman's sweater, doe-colored trousers and soft black leather loafers. On his gold watch chain dangled a Phi Beta Kappa key and around his neck was a medal—embossed with a portrait of John Rutledge—that had been given him by a governor of South Carolina.

Dickey struck it rich a few years ago with a novel called *Deliverance*, but he is also the author of seven books of poetry, one of which—*Buckdancer's Choice*—won a National Book Award in 1967. He feels that his fellow poets have never forgiven him for the success of *Deliverance*. "I don't carry literary grudges," he said, sprawled across his bed with a beer can in his hand, "but American poets are like crabs in a bucket. When one crawls up, the others try to pull him down. I just pay them no mind and go on about my business."

The Zodiac, Dickey's most ambitious poem to date, has been on his mind since he was a student at Vanderbilt in the late 1940s. He had read a poem with the same title by a Dutch poet, Hendrik Marsman, who was lost at sea when his ship was torpedoed in 1940. "It was a poem in twelve sections, poorly translated, about a Dutch sailor who returns home, maybe to die, and who tries desperately with the help of aquavit to relate himself to the universe. The stars are his link, and he uses them the way a navigator would. My version has very little to do with Marsman's. You might call it an homage to a man I know very little about. His idea stuck with me not because of the poem itself but because it was a great idea that someone should do right. It's the ultimate poem, the link between the mind of the poet and God, who is a poet, an attempt to find the ultimate secret of God through the stars, which speak the language of God.

"Of course, when you try to write the ultimate poem you fail, but I like to think your failure is your success. I wanted to get in something of the fury and creative ecstasy that make a poet take on something like this. You shouldn't be expected to take on projects so huge, but poets do it all the time, poets who try to do the same thing God did in creating the universe.

"But to try, when my sailor in the poem and I try, you sometimes have to down a lot of alcohol. Someone told me the other day that *The Zodiac* is nothing but the glorification of a drunken poet. It ain't. It's just about a poet who uses drink like a medicine. I don't think I should turn loose a poem until I've given it a long and honorable fight. At the point at which I can't think of a change for the better I let a poem go. I've been fighting with this one for a good long time.

"What I really wanted to put across is what Samuel Beckett says at the end of *The Unnamable*: 'I can't go on, I'll go on.' That's the essential feeling of a poet. There's always hope, you see. *The Zodiac* is my poetry shot at the best-seller list. That's hope for you." (1977)

HARLAN ELLISON

Harlan Ellison was on the
telephone from Los Angeles, and we were making arrange-
ments to meet during one of his rare visits to New York.
"Would you recognize me if you saw me?" he asked. "No," I
said. "I'm 44 years old, five-feet-five, and I look like I'm ready
for a fight."

Now, having met him, I couldn't think of a better description. Mention the name Harlan Ellison to most readers
and the immediate reaction would probably be "science-
fiction writer," a reaction that couldn't displease Ellison
more. "It's like being called a nigger," he says. With over 900
short stories to his credit, along with thirty-two books and
dozens of screenplays and television scripts (including a few
Star Trek episodes), Ellison claims that he has never written
science fiction. "I'm a fantasy writer, a magic realist like
Borges, Nabokov, Vonnegut or William Kotzwinkle, and I'm
sick of being tarred with the science-fiction brush. Science
fiction is only a category to help bookstore owners arrange
their stock."

His new collection of short stories, *Strange Wine: Fifteen
New Stories from the Nightside of the World*, would be a
difficult one to squeeze onto any science-fiction shelf. It ranges
from ghost stories to revenge yarns to a demonic alphabet
("A is for Atlantean," with a short tale to go with it, "B is for
Breathdeath," and so on) to pointedly vindictive literary
satire. One story deals with the grotesque deaths of a paper-
back-book editor and a Manhattan bookstore buyer who
weren't up on what was or was not science fiction.

"Most science-fiction fans like to think of themselves
as special people," Ellison says. "They especially like to
picture themselves as being on top of the latest issues, but
most of them are reactionary escapists. The average fan probably started as a high school misfit who discovered pulp
magazines as a way of avoiding reality. As for the writers,

there is an old-boy network of them who make a big deal out of being unrecognized, the way New Yorkers take pride in surviving muggings."

As promotional and charity stunts Ellison has written stories in store windows in London, Boston and Los Angeles, but he says he does his best work in his hilltop house just off Mulholland Drive in the middle of Los Angeles. "I left New York in 1962 with my head full of visions of Bill Holden floating face down in Gloria Swanson's swimming pool. Hollywood was the place everyone went to die. But I love the place. I'll never leave." He also took up darts in California, a game he is now fanatical about. "The way to pick up girls was to go to bars, and since I don't drink I played darts." Whether or not the ploy worked, Ellison describes his marital status this way: "Four marriages, four divorces, no children, no alimony."

But always, with Ellison, the conversation kept coming back to science fiction. "I was in Paris working on a movie, and they gave a party for me. Alain Resnais—you know, *Last Year at Marienbad*—came. As soon as he saw me he kissed me three times, not twice, and said that my work was a glorious combination of James Joyce and James Cagney. I was so dumbstruck all I could think of doing was asking if I could quote that on a book jacket. 'A glorious combination....' And where do they stick me? With all those *pishers* on the science-fiction shelf. Sometimes I get scared that I'm going to die in the midst of a story and one of those guys is going to finish it for me." (1978)

Buchi Emecheta is well named. It is a name that captures her spirit of hard-working independence. In Ibo, she says, "Buchi" means "You are not my god" (the inference being "So you can't tell me what to do"). "Emecheta" means "If you do good you will get a reward." When she was 18 she and her husband left Nigeria to live in London. By the time she was 21, her husband had abandoned her and their five children. "So I wrote," she recalls. "I wrote to get the anger out of me." At first it was a diary, which ran in *The New Statesman.* Since then it has been novels, four so far, the most recent being *The Joys of Motherhood.* "My oldest daughter is now 17. In the old times she would be old enough to take care of me," she says with a laugh, "but I am still writing, and I think I will keep on."

During her recent lecture tour of the United States, her first, she said she thought of her novels as ballads. "I grew up in Lagos," she said, "but I was lucky in the summers and was sent to live with my grandmother in Ibuza. She told the old stories, actually she sang them as long ballads. I think I do the same in my novels. I know I am doing the same in a new series of short books Oxford University is publishing for Nigerian children. In them I pass on to city children a sense of the old ways, just as my grandmother did."

American readers may find it difficult to think of *The Joys of Motherhood* in such lyrical terms. It is a strong, austerely told story of a woman who goes from her tribal village to the city and literally gives her life to her children.

Buchi Emecheta speaks three African dialects but writes in English. "I translate in my mind," she says. "From my grandmother I learned ballads, but from my mother I learned cunning. My younger brother was sent off to school because he was a boy, and I stayed at home and was given simple lessons in reading and arithmetic, which cost my parents only ten cents a month. But I was clever and won a scholarship to a boarding school that was built for the daughters of English civil servants." Today, her brother is an accountant in Lagos and she lectures on West

African literature and women's studies at the University of London. "We go back to Africa to visit but my children become too frightened by all the noise. I am afraid they are becoming too English."   (1980)

MARIAN ENGEL

Every country has its ration of hardworking, serious novelists who turn out a steady stream of solid, well-reviewed books but never win much of a readership. In *Who's Afraid of Canadian Culture?* S. M. Crean mentions Marian Engel of Toronto as a serious novelist most Canadians have never heard of, even though since 1968 she has published four novels and a collection of short stories. Marian Engel might have been unknown last year, but this year she published her sixth novel, *Bear*, and it has been on best-seller lists all over Canada.

Nationalists have found deep meanings in it concerning Canadians' relationship with the land they live on. Jungians have seen it as a mythic tale. Feminists have praised its insights into female sexuality. As for Marian Engel, she said the other day, "I think of it more as just a love story." It is a love story, the story of a young historical researcher and her unexpected relationship with a bear in northern Ontario.

"The idea just jumped out at me," Miss Engel says, "but I wasn't going to do anything about it since I knew almost nothing about bears. I told some friends of mine in the Writers' Union about it, and they all started telling bear stories. I've discovered—and it's still happening—that all you have to do is say 'bear' to a storyteller and all kinds of tales come pouring out. Then someone said I'd never be able to pull off a love story between a woman and a bear. So I had to do it, and I just marched off and did it."

Lou, the researcher, encounters her bear when she is sent off to catalog the library in a mansion on a river island deep in the woods. The mansion, oddly enough, is an octagon built according to the rules of Orson Squire Fowler, the 19th-century American publisher who was a zealous advocate of phrenology and the healthful qualities of octagonal houses. Fowler, Lou comments, "was the kind of American we were all warned about."

Miss Engel became curious about Fowler after inheriting some books that belonged to her great-grandfather. "Stuck into the books I found a lot of little notes on Fowler and on other subjects, such as Swedish coal production and Bright's disease. When it came time for me to put a building on the island in *Bear*, I first used a huge stone castle, but Gothic castles are getting pretty common in fiction these days and this one had to be special. So I built a classic Fowler octagon. Also, I was sorry that my great-grandfather's notes never cohered. I kept hoping they would, but they were just notes about whatever he was reading. One of the nice things about writing fiction is that you can make a world that does cohere, so I made all the notes that fall out of the books in *Bear* be about bears."

A point she also makes in the novel is that Canadians live two lives "of completely different quality," winter lives and summer lives. "We shuck off all our earnestness in the summer. There's optimism and joy in the summer and then the mists close in again in October and we get gloomy. I was living in England when people started going to Ingmar Bergman movies. Everyone kept praising all that moodiness as being very Scandinavian. I kept thinking it was all very Canadian."

She says she was nervous about what the reaction to *Bear* might be. "I was afraid the neighbors would chase my twin daughters down the street shouting at them that their mother wrote dirty books. People seem to really like it even though they tend to avoid talking about the bear itself. If I mention him, they just smile."   (1977)

WILLARD R. ESPY

At a time when half the publishers in New York seem to be rushing out guidebooks on how to trace lost or forgotten family roots, Willard R. Espy has come up with an unabashed celebration of the Espys of Oysterville, state of Washington, a family that seems to have forgotten few of its roots and enjoys nothing more than talking about them.

Espy, who looks as though he might have stepped out of a *Punch* cartoon by Ronald Searle (in fact, for two years he wrote a regular column for that British magazine), calls his book *Oysterville: Roads to Grandpa's Village.* "It *was* my grandfather's village," he said the other day. "He founded it in the 1850s, and he felt the place was his responsibility, the whole family did, still does. It is an isolated place on a peninsula just north of the Columbia River, and when you grew up there you were growing up literally at the end of the world. To amuse ourselves we read a lot—more for quantity than quality—and talked about the early days of the village and how my grandfather teamed up with the local Indians to harvest oysters and ship them off to San Francisco, where people had more money than they knew what to do with.

"There would be arguments that lasted weeks over, say, whether or not my grandfather carried the family's beehive clock all the way from Pennsylvania. My father and Aunt Dora claimed he did, but my Uncle Will and Uncle Cecil said he lost everything when a fire burned his Conestoga wagon somewhere near Fort Laramie. I still have the clock, by the way. It's decorated with a painting of a red and yellow bird. The odd thing was that there was little interest in family history before my grandfather headed West. We knew there was an Alexander Hamilton back there somewhere, and we all assumed that he was *the* Alexander Hamilton. I've since found that he wasn't."

Willard Espy came East in 1932 to make his way as a

freelance writer and public relations man. In 1935 he found himself out of work and to pass the time he wrote to as many elderly relatives as he could locate and asked them about the family. He's been working on that project ever since. "I caught a lot of them just in time," he recalls. "Many of them could still remember their parents' and grandparents' tales of the Civil War and even the Revolution. In all I was able to catalog some 600 direct ancestors. I was also helped by the fact that we were a family of scribblers. I have about a four-foot shelf of family notes."

Among ancestors he uncovered were a woman who was hanged as a witch in Salem, Massachusetts ("Those witchcraft trials were a class thing," Espy believes. "It was the poor against the rich"), a Confederate captain who was so outraged by the way the Civil War ended that he packed himself off to exile in Mexico, a preacher who sailed around Cape Horn to save souls in the California gold fields and a liberal sprinkling of gleeful Indian killers.

But holding everything together in his book are memories of Oysterville. The town—which houses about thirty families including that of Espy's sister—has recently been named a National Historical Site by the federal government. Espy is now afraid the place is going to be overrun with tourists and delights in a sign he had put up. It reads "This Way to the Beach" and it points away from the village. He still visits there two or three times a year and says he has been spending the last seven years trying fruitlessly to build "the perfect croquet court" on its sandy soil.

"The townspeople have been quite kindly to the Espys," he says. "They've put up with a lot of pretension from the lords of the manor. I suspect, though, that they chuckle a good deal about us in their beds at night."

Two closing points: *Oysterville*, with its many drawings by Earl Thollander, is a beautifully designed and printed book. And, finally, Willard Espy hates oysters. "As a kid I was drowned in them. We seemed to have them for every meal. Even oyster pie. I can't stand the sight of the damned things."

(1977)

JOHN FOWLES

The English novelist John Fowles is in the unusual position of being more popular abroad than he is at home. *The Collector*, *The Magus* and particularly *The French Lieutenant's Woman* sold well in Britain, but were nothing like the successes they were in North America. There was even a marked increase in tourism in the seaside town of Lyme Regis, the setting for *The French Lieutenant's Woman*, after the novel was published in the United States.

Fowles claims to be especially bemused by the following he has among American academics. "The thesis writers," he says, "are after me. They demand that I have some sort of 'plan' to my work. Actually, I write without calculation. If you write in a complicated way, you can't think you musn't write in the complicated way just because it encourages academics who would be better occupied raking leaves."

Fowles has now published his first book of short stories, *The Ebony Tower*, and a lot of leaves are guaranteed to go unraked. The book consists of four longish short stories and a translation of a 12th-century tale by Marie de France. It is in the "Personal Note" that leads off the translation that Fowles delivers the zinger that will be heard on a thousand campuses: "The working title of this collection was *Variations*, by which I meant to suggest variations on certain themes in previous books of mine and methods of narrative presentation."

So, the rush is on to track down those variations. Readers who claim to find the Greek philosopher Heraclitus ("It is not possible to step twice in the same river") as the secret to the Fowles riddle will find a number of Heraclitean rivers to ponder. And remember the curious double ending to *The French Lieutenant's Woman*? Compare that to the ending of the next to the last story in *The Ebony Tower*. And that novel a girl in the first story is reading, isn't it *The Magus*?

58.

It is indeed, and Fowles admits that's a little joke of his, "to get at California kids who insist on reading the novel as an astrological work."

All of which may be great sport, but the reader shouldn't overlook just how good the individual stories are, especially the title story, which has to do with a young British art critic who visits an aging expatriate painter in Brittany and encounters the painter's two lovely sleep-in companions.

The short-story form is a new one for Fowles and he says he enjoys it chiefly because "it's so pleasant being able to finish something." *The Ebony Tower*, in fact, was written as a change of pace while Fowles was at work on a novel—"a very long novel dealing with the nature of Englishness"—that won't be finished for another two years, at least. And after that? "What I would really like to do," he says, with a conspiratorial wink, "is to try my hand at science fiction." (1975)

CARLOS FUENTES

Whwhen novelist Carlos Fuentes arrived at the Elysée Palace in 1975 to present his credentials as the new Mexican ambassador to Valéry Giscard d'Estaing, the French president greeted him by saying, "How I wish I could be a novelist." To which, as Fuentes recalls it, he would like to have said, "How I wish I could be president of France."

Tall, lean, urbane, Fuentes is, in fact, the very model of the modern French president of the Giscard stripe. And he is no stranger to politics. "In Mexico," he says, "I'm

panned or praised for political reasons, not literary ones."
In the United States—he spent much of the past year in
Princeton, New Jersey—he has had a running battle with the
State Department over his leftist sympathies.

Fuentes' new novel, *The Hydra Head*—part spy thriller,
part slapstick comedy, part homage to American detective
novels and movies of the 1940s—is very much a political
portrait of Mexico City today. "The one thing you can bank
on in the novel," he says, "is that no one is telling the truth.
That's something I learned from Dashiell Hammett."

Fuentes sees his book as a return to his own territory.
"Twenty years ago I wrote a Mexico City novel called *Where
the Air Is Clear*, and now I've come back for another look at
a place that has a strong sense of humiliation and inferiority.
Mexico is a land that has been humiliated and slapped around
for years. France once invaded because a mob sacked a French
bakery in Vera Cruz. Today, the United States talks of building a Berlin Wall along the border. But the recent oil discoveries may change all this. Mexico will no longer have
poverty as an excuse for failure.

"We are a country that builds monuments to losers.
That, too, must change. There is a vacant traffic circle on the
Reforma in Mexico City, and we should put a statue of Cortés
there. Until we recognize that we are children of both Spain,
the conquerors, and the Indians, the defeated, we will be living
in a homemade ghetto."

But Fuentes seems more interested in Latin American
unity than in Mexican nationalism. "I would rather," he says,
"be thought of as a Latin American writer than a Mexican.
Our unity is our language and our culture. Our division is
our politics. My father was a diplomat, and I never really saw
Mexico City until I was 15. It was a shock, but I could see the
place in proportion with fresh eyes. I can still see Mexico
better from the outside.

"Latin America is one of the great poles of narration
today. We have a great need to set it all down and say it all.
If a novelist doesn't say it, who will? A politician? Hardly."

(1979)

60.

JOHN GARDNER

Afew years ago, in a church basement in an upstate New York river town, I heard John Gardner give a revival sermon that was a stem-winder. Actually, the sermon was one of his short stories, and the church was a university chapel, but the reading had all the intensity of Jonathan Edwards railing away at sinners in the hands of an angry God.

Well, Gardner is at it again. In his new book-length essay, *On Moral Fiction*, he says flatly: "True art is moral: it seeks to improve life, not debase it. It seeks to hold off, at least for awhile, the twilight of the gods and us. . . . It may joke, or mock, or while away the time. But trivial art has no meaning or value except in the shadow of more serious art, the kind of art that beats back the monsters and, if you will, makes the world safe for triviality. That art that tends toward destruction . . . is not properly art at all."

For the past year Gardner has been living in Baltimore, and at 45 his hair is longer and whiter than ever. His laugh—he laughs a lot, almost as punctuation—is becoming a bit rueful. With over a dozen novels (*October Light*, 1976, is the most recent), story collections, children's books and books of Chaucer criticism to his credit, he seems to have reached a time for taking stock. "My position is not Christian," he said on a recent visit to New York with his teenage son. "It's simpler than that. Art, like medicine, should support what's healthy. It shouldn't support despair. Is that old hat? Of course it is, outrageously so. We're getting so caught up in our complete moral corruption that we can't see what's happening. Too many writers—and especially too many that live around New York City—have reached the point where they can't seem to even hear arguments against despair."

After stoking up his pipe, he continues. "We've reached the point where the entertainers—the writers of mysteries, spy stories, even nurse books—are head and shoulders above the serious writers. I'm not against them. We need the side-shows to point the way to the main tent, but people are confusing the sideshows with the main tent."

Authors who don't pass the Gardner test include John Barth, John Updike, Joseph Heller, E. L. Doctorow, Coover, Crews, Mailer, Roth, Vonnegut. Those on the short approved list include Malamud (sometimes), Cheever (not as often), Joyce Carol Oates (for a few short stories only), Eudora Welty (only for *Losing Battles*). His two favorite current writers are John Fowles (especially for *Daniel Martin*) and John Irving (especially for *The World According to Garp*).

"We have to have models to live by," Gardner continues, "and artists are the ones to provide them, artists and maybe saints whose lives are their art. Fiction is characters, and you have to have them firmly in mind before you write. You have to imagine their doing all kinds of things you don't actually have them do in your novel. You begin by copying people you know, and later you invent characters and get deeper into them than anyone you can ever know.

"You have to make a passionate affirmation without oversimplifying. It can't be just intellect. In fact, I suspect we turn on the intellect only when we're in trouble, to figure out what went wrong."

Although Gardner claims that "good art projects a sense of peace," he does not find writing fiction a peaceful process. "Ruminating and milling make a novel," he says. "I have to have it all in my head before I write it down, and I have too much energy to do that sitting down. So, I ride horses and walk. Lately, I've been doing a lot of walking."   (1978)

JAMES M. GAVIN

James M. Gavin is a general who believes war too serious a matter to be left to generals. In his new book, *On to Berlin*, which follows his career as a World War II airborne commander from North Africa through Sicily, Salerno, Normandy, Nijmegen and the Bulge to Berlin, he makes a strong case for his opinion that the war in Europe might have been shorter, and Berlin might have been saved from the Russians, had the State Department formulated some policy on how the war should end.

Gavin is no stranger to the State Department, having served as President Kennedy's ambassador to France for two years. "When I was writing the book," he said during a recent visit to New York from his home outside Boston, "I asked State if they could show me what memos they had on the outcome of the war and the state of Berlin. They couldn't come up with a single scrap of paper."

In 1944 Gavin at 37 was the youngest American general since the Civil War. "It wasn't all that hard," he says. "I was a parachutist who survived. You don't find many old parachutists."

As the result of one combat landing, Gavin's left leg is half an inch shorter than his right. "The advantage of being an airborne commander is that you are dressed exactly the same as your men. To do your job you have to carry the same equipment as they do and be where they are." He is disdainful of officers who led from command posts well behind the lines, and, although he is loath to say so, he is disdainful of Eisenhower, who was rarely where his men were.

"A B.S. degree from West Point doesn't qualify a man to know what is going on in battle. You have to be there. You have to smell it. If an officer hangs around the command post too long, he begins to dress for other officers. When he gets to the front he can't get along with the men. Lord Moran,

Churchill's doctor, once said that courage was like a bank account. It can be overdrawn. An officer has to be there to know when that time comes."

Patton, obviously, is Gavin's hero. "The great tragedy," he says, "is that for the second half of the war we weren't using our greatest general." Oddly enough, he feels kindly toward Patton's archenemy, Field Marshal Montgomery. "I liked him and felt sorry for him. He had to clear everything every day with Churchill, and Churchill made it clear that Britain had to be in the center of things even if it meant sacrificing Americans."

There is a final point the general especially wanted to make. "There is a myth that the Germans were the better soldiers and that we won because we were better equipped. We weren't better equipped. We never did develop a bazooka that worked. When we jumped into Sicily my men were young kids right out of Fort Benning. They hit the Hermann Goering Division, the best Germany had to offer, and we made them run. We made them run."   (1978)

ALLEN GINSBERG

Someone has annotated Allen Ginsberg, and Allen Ginsberg couldn't be happier. Actually, of course, it was the poet's words that were annotated, tape recordings made as he toured the United States in the spring of 1971, lecturing on campuses, talking with other poets in classroom situations, answering the questions of students or anyone with a question to ask. The annotations were made by Gordon Ball, a graduate student at the University of North Carolina who was along on the tour and who has provided enough footnotes, reading lists and indexes to delight anyone who delights in scholarly apparatus.

What delights Ginsberg about the book, entitled *Allen Verbatim*, is that it provides outsiders "an opportunity to eavesdrop on counterculture intellectual life." Back in New York City recently after a long stay in the West, Ginsberg said, "There is a myth that Jack Kerouac, William Burroughs and myself are anti-intellectual. That's not true. We're a university of our own, an alternative academy, and this book gives insight into the forms and disciplines I'm into. It is the record of one season's interests and contains everything from gnostic philosophy to discussions of prosody to nasty political secrets."

To be more specific, it is the record of Ginsberg's views on subjects that range from Ezra Pound's economic theories (which Ginsberg agrees with) to Blake's mysticism to how to harness the energy of the ocean's tides to how to stop drug addiction (get the junkies out of the hands of the police and into the hands of doctors) to the role of the CIA in the international drug trade ("The CIA is a major dope dealer in Asia; it works with the Mafia and at some point *becomes* the Mafia").

One remarkable thing about *Allen Verbatim* is that although Ginsberg has published over a dozen books since *Howl* appeared in 1956 (including *The Fall of America*, which was the winner of a 1974 National Book Award for Poetry), this is the first time he has published a book with a commercial publisher. All his books until now have been brought out by small presses, chiefly by Lawrence Ferlinghetti's City Lights Books in San Francisco.

Ginsberg says this has been deliberate on his part. He likes small presses because he believes in decentralized publishing. He says, "It isn't healthy for publishing, or for poetry, to have large New York houses dominate the scene." He especially likes City Lights because he sees it as part of a great "bohemian family." Ferlinghetti is not only a publisher but also a poet himself, and Ginsberg is especially happy that the success of his books (and they are successful; City Lights has sold more than 300,000 copies of *Howl* alone) helps bankroll the publication of other poets.

While talking with Ginsberg one can't help but be impressed with his sense of poetic missionary work. The $8000 or so he makes in royalties each year from City Lights, he says, is all he needs to live on. "Years ago I took a vow of relative penury, and I know how to live cheap." His major expense is the farm—he calls it a poetry commune—he owns in Otsego County, New York. Ginsberg himself doesn't live there, but he sees it as a "refuge for used poets," especially for a number of young poets who are involved with the St. Mark's Poetry Project on Manhattan's Lower East Side. "If you are not sick, the farm is a good place to meditate," he says. "If you are sick, well, it is a good place for that, too."

It is a working farm, largely self-sustaining and non-electrified, but to pay the mortgage or to raise money for other projects (many having to do with the establishment of Buddhist centers) or to simply pay the dentist bills, he goes on the sort of lecture tour documented in *Allen Verbatim*. From these, he says, he raises as much as $30,000 a year.

Getting back to the myth that Ginsberg is anti-intellectual, he said, "I've been too busy writing to do the kind of teaching and explaining less active poets get involved in. When all my poetry is assembled into one book, it is going to add up to about 2000 pages. The assembled prose will be longer. It is all now just coming together, and when it gets rolling it's going to be pretty impressive. The literary world is going to have to contend with us, whether they like it or not." (1975)

Since 1942 the Carey-Thomas Award has been given annually to an American publisher for doing something out of the ordinary, "for a distinguished project of book publishing," to quote *Publishers Weekly*, the award's sponsor. This year, for the first time, it was awarded to a library, New York's Pierpont Morgan Library. The "distinguished project" is a lavishly illustrated book entitled *Early Children's Books and Their Illustration*, which the Morgan published in cooperation with the Boston publisher David R. Godine.

I went down to the Morgan the other day to talk with Gerald Gottlieb, the library's Curator of Early Children's Books and the author of the prizewinning book. He was at his desk at one end of the baronial reading room, surrounded by a magnificent clutter of frail books and pamphlets. He introduced me to a young woman working with him, a graduate student at NYU's Institute of Fine Arts. "The Morgan Library," he said, "has undoubtedly the largest collection of early children's books in the Western Hemisphere—almost 15,000 items—and it has never been completely cataloged. We're finding new things all the time."

He picked up a small book with a marbled jacket. "Here's a typical 18th-century work for children." It was called *Little Truths Better than Great Fables*, and included lessons on how to make paper and observations on the habits of blind people and the need for charity. It was published in London in 1787. "They believed that little truths were indeed better than great fables. Fairy stories, ballads about Robin Hood and all that sort of thing were thought to be unsuitable for children. They survived, in print at least, as street literature, broadsides that were hawked for a penny and then more often than not thrown away.

"The idea of children reading for enjoyment and not for

instruction is really a late development. Partly because of the high rate of infant mortality, it was thought that children should be prepared as soon as possible to face death. Their souls had to be made ready. It was immoral to waste that precious time on entertainment. If they survived there would be time enough for that later. The children, though, found their own books and took them over. *Pilgrim's Progress*, for instance. After a diet of grammars, prayers and moral instructions, the book was a revelation. John Bunyan didn't set out to entertain, but he did. Also, later, there was *Robinson Crusoe*. Reread it sometime; it's full of pious sermons on Christian duty, but any kid who ever played alone would have to love it."

An important part of *Early Children's Books*, and the exhibit on which it was based, was Gottlieb's search for the roots of children's literature in early non-children's books. "Many scholars are myopic," he says, "about seeing the origins of children's literature in pre-18th-century books." He uses *Aesop's Fables* as an example. This was one of the first printed books, one of the first illustrated books and one of the most frequently illustrated books, but it was not until the late 18th century that the fables were actually published in an edition for children.

By the end of the 18th century children's books had become more commonplace and less didactic. Even such adult books as *Tom Jones* and *Fanny Hill* appeared in abridgments for children. "They were lucrative sidelines for printers," Gottlieb says, "but they were toys. No one took care to preserve them. They weren't expected to survive, and most of them didn't. Authors who wrote for children did so anonymously or pseudonymously. Oliver Goldsmith was one of the first well-known authors to sign his children's books, but he only acknowledged the serious ones. The less serious ones, he didn't. Very few scholars have tried to track down the 'lost' children's books of well-known 18th-century writers. But then, very little is really known about early children's books. No matter where you look, you make discoveries.

"That was one of the joys of putting together the material for the exhibit and the book. You don't expect to find a lot of humor in a place like the Morgan Library. But it's here, and it was fun discovering it."   (1976)

GÜNTER GRASS

When it came time to translate *The Flounder*, Günter Grass's first major novel in fifteen years, Grass and nine translators from countries that ranged from Japan to Israel to Sweden met together for a week in the country outside Frankfurt. (Ralph Manheim, the English-language translator, didn't attend.) "For one week," Grass said during a recent visit to New York, "they asked me questions and I told them stories. When it was all over I cooked them up a nice fish soup, made of seven different kinds of fish from the North Sea and the Baltic."

The meal was an apt conclusion, for *The Flounder* is one of the gargantuan fish stories of all time, an outsized, raucous attempt to tell the story of mankind, from the Neolithic swamp dweller on the shores of the Vistula to the modern globetrotting German novelist, all from the point of view of one man . . . with a little help from a fish.

"People need books with an epic background," Grass says. "They are bored with books that tell only one story on one level. They need something fantastic, something that gives them a sense of living in history. As it is, most novels aren't giving readers a chance to use their sense of fantasy."

Grass began *The Flounder* just after the German elections in 1972. "I'd been campaigning for months for the Social Democrats," he recalls. "I was making three to five speeches a day, and it got so I couldn't hear the language for all the rhetoric. I had become lost in a secondhand language and was afraid I was going to lose track of the real thing. I knew I had to write something big, and since I was five years away from my 50th birthday I decided to spend the time on a big novel for my 50th birthday present."

Grass made his mark on the world's literary scene in 1959 with *The Tin Drum*. Since then he has published three other novels, several plays and a few nonfiction works. "I never graduated from high school," he says. "Perhaps that's why I write so much. Maybe I have to prove myself. Still, when I write a sentence it isn't as long as the usual German long sentence. I can say in five words what it takes most Germans twelve words to say."

Grass left school at 15 and was drafted into the Army at 16. A year later he was wounded in Czechoslovakia and captured by the Americans. "It was only then that I discovered modern American literature, Hemingway and Faulkner and the rest. It all came in a rush, but my favorites are still Melville and Mark Twain."

Part of the profits on *The Flounder* (it sold 300,000 copies in three months in Germany) have been set aside by Grass to establish a literary prize in honor of the expressionist novelist Alfred Döblin (*Alexanderplatz, Berlin*, 1931). "He was my teacher," Grass says, "although I never met him. The prize will be given each year to an epic manuscript. A big novel, a complex translation, but nothing small. I was lucky in that I grew up in Danzig. Since it was a free city the Nazis didn't get there until 1939, after they had destroyed the culture of the rest of Germany. What we need to do now is reestablish a literary tradition in Germany. Perhaps my Döblin Prize will help." (1979)

Red Grooms, a big ginger-haired kid from Nashville, arrived in New York City in the late 1950s and soon made his name in the downtown art world by organizing some of the earliest "happenings" (Pasty Man, a happy pyromaniac, was one of his favorite creations) and by wearing spectacularly paint-spattered clothes. An artist who knew him then recalls, "We all spilled paint, but Red . . . you could spot him a block away."

Grooms has never lost his sense of theater. In 1961 he and his wife, Mimi, toured northern Italy by horse and wagon, giving shadow-puppet shows en route. "Just like *La Strada*," Grooms recalls, "Mimi and I and an English kid who played banjo went from Florence to Venice and back again, although we never made it to the Lido. They wouldn't let our horse on the boat." Later, back in New York, Red began building small dioramas that mixed painting, cartoons and papier-mâché figures. One of the first was an open-sided reproduction of a lively dinner party at the Groomses' loft. "It took seven months to make," Red says, "and all my friends thought I'd lost my mind." Today, *Loft on 26th Street* is in the Hirsh-horn Museum in Washington, D.C.

The models soon grew in size, and Grooms made up the name "sculpto-picto-ramas" for them. *The City of Chicago*, a collage of street scenes, gangsters, bridges and a Mayor Daley of King Kong proportions, is 25 feet square. *The Great American Rodeo*, commissioned by the Fort Worth Art Museum and complete with fourteen cowboys and cowgirls and a Brahman bull, is 100 feet wide and 30 feet deep. Grooms's masterpiece, his Sistine Chapel, is *Ruckus Manhattan*, a manic, walk-through re-creation of New York from the Statue of Liberty (which sports red platform shoes and a lighted cigar) to Rockefeller Center. *Ruckus'* history—from an early tryout in 1975 in an empty Wall Street storefront to the un-veiling of its full, tacky glory at the staid Marlborough

Gallery on West Fifty-seventh Street in 1976—is now told with a brief text and ninety-eight black-and-white and color photographs in *Red Grooms and Ruckus Manhattan*, by Judd Tully.

The "sculptural novel," as Grooms likes to call *Ruckus*, was swarmed over by 50,000 people downtown and 100,000 uptown, and as a fan who saw it in both places I can testify that it was the greatest show in town. There was a narrow, twisted Wall Street with Trinity Church at its head and there were the 27-feet-tall twin towers of the World Trade Center. Also a ferry boat that tipped alarmingly, an overwrought Brooklyn Bridge, crazed cooks in Chinatown, a full-size subway car and a Forty-second Street porno shop.

"We built it in a year," Grooms said the other day, "and it was pure panic all the way. Oddly enough, or maybe not, journalists and children seemed to like it the most. When we began it we wanted to do a complete novelization of the city, but that was impossible. We didn't use blueprints. We just sketched away and dragged in more paint and lumber until we were finished. It was supposed to look as though it was a fantasy we had just scribbled out, but fantasy based on our firsthand knowledge of the neighborhoods."

Grooms, with Mimi and their work crew, built their version of the World Trade Center before the original was completed. "The real building was empty and boring," he says. "There was no nostalgia about the place like there had been when we'd done the Woolworth Building, so we made up our own with Henry Hudson riding a working elevator and alligators dancing around underneath. The fun of the show was doing the details. We didn't actually do as many people as I wanted, but once the show opened and the visitors crowded in, they became the people. After they left at night the place seemed downright eerie."

Grooms works alone now. He and Mimi split up not long after they crated *Ruckus Manhattan* in the fall of 1976 and put it into storage. "I'm painting again," he says, "working small, just for myself, and it's a relief. At the height of activity on *Ruckus* I had twenty-five people working for me.

"But I know I'm only marking time until *Ruckus Manhattan* comes out of storage again. I'm like Dr. Frankenstein. The monster's going to get out, and I'm the one who will have to deal with it. In looking back, I think I was misled by world's fairs. I've always liked them, but there comes a time when they just fall apart and disintegrate. The same with my stuff. *Ruckus Manhattan* could be set up again and opened to the public like a boardwalk wax museum, and I'd like that. It might hold together for six months that way and then it would be gone, like, you know, cotton candy that just falls apart."

(1978)

TOM T. HALL

"The frightening thing about writing books," Tom T. Hall said the other day, "is that there are so many people who can read." Hall is a Nashville songwriter who has been turning out a steady supply of words and music since the early 1960s. He first made it big when Jeannie C. Riley recorded his "Harper Valley PTA" and then went on to make a name for himself as a singer with such songs as "Love Is" and "The Year That Clayton Delaney Died." Because so many of his songs have plots, Tex Ritter called him "The Storyteller," and the name stuck. Hall has just written his first book, *The Storyteller's Nashville.*

"I got so tired reading magazine articles based on somebody's weekend in Nashville, I decided to tell what the place was like to live in full time," he said during his annual New York visit to perform at the Lone Star Cafe. "I decided to use my own story as a guide to the town." It is a likable, low-keyed tale peopled not so much by celebrities as by barroom acquaintances with stories to tell.

"I avoid saloon work these days," he says. "They are an occupational hazard, and I'm the only country singer I know that's been thrown out of a place he was appearing in. That happened in Phoenix. Sometimes I think 80 percent of the people in this business get themselves killed on the highway before they ever get to Nashville. And for the rest, the great challenge is keeping out of the paper-slipper academy. The crackup rate is so terrifying no one talks about it. So I take off from December to April every year just to write songs."

Songwriting, Hall feels, should be a full-time job. "A lot of songs never get written because successful songwriters have made it sound too easy. You've got to get up early a lot of mornings before you have a hit. When you think of all those guys just waiting for a song to come to them, you better start thinking of songs they're wasting."

One of Hall's most creative sidelines is his children's songs, usually about animals. "Kids like me," he says. "Their parents bring them to my concerts, and I look out and see a bunch of 10-year-olds singing 'I Like Beer' along with me and loving it. That doesn't seem right, so I wrote some songs, like 'Sneaky Snake,' for them."

What he calls his philosophy of life, though, appears in one of his adult songs: "Ain't but three things in this world/ that's worth a solitary dime,/ But old dogs and children and watermelon wine." He adds, "One old man I heard about even had that sung at his funeral." (1980)

"Sex," says Eleanor Hamilton, "is one of the few skills people learn through talk and not demonstration. Can you imagine what it would be like if a couple of nervous parents sat their child down in the living room and tried to *explain* how to swim?" At 68 years of age, Dr. Hamilton, the mother of four children, has been a teacher, a marriage counselor, a sex therapist and an author (*Sex and Sexuality, Sex Before Marriage*). She has just published a guide for young people, *Sex, with Love*, which she talked about recently at her rustic brookside home in southwestern Massachusetts.

"Never before," she said, "have we had to solve some of the sexual problems we now face. Until just a few years ago the average girl matured at age 15 and married at age 18. Now they are maturing at 12 and marrying at 22. Ten years between maturity and matrimony is too long for a bodily process to go without functioning. No one should lay his or her sexuality away in cold storage for as long as that. Without function there is dysfunction. There has to be a moral and safe way to express that sexuality. And it must be done in an atmosphere of mutual love and trust."

What Dr. Hamilton suggests is a program of heavy petting, masturbation—"an ugly word for a pleasant act"—and massage. "There's lots of sexuality that isn't intercourse," she says. "I don't think most young people are ready for intercourse until they are at least 17, probably older. In all my years as a therapist I haven't seen a case in which two kids, together, could both handle the responsibility, and it is a responsibility that both partners have to take. I think, in fact, that it is a relief to most young people not to be pressured into 'going all the way.'"

The age barrier is only one of Dr. Hamilton's "minimum requirements" for intercourse. Some of the others include training in birth control ("The moment the idea of intercourse crosses a girl's mind she should receive instruction, if only to file away somewhere"); preparedness—both emotional and financial—to deal with pregnancy in case there is an accident in birth control; emotional and guiltless commitment; and a protected and pleasant environment ("not the backseat of a car").

"The idea is to control sex," she adds, "not repress it. As a sex counselor I've found that the most difficult question to get an answer to is: What are your fantasies? People are afraid of their fantasies largely because they seem so bizarre. People fantasize things they would never think of actually doing and that gets the juices flowing. But there is often guilt involved. I sometimes think that 50 percent of the people getting psychiatric help wouldn't need it if only they got over their hang-ups about masturbation."

Sex, with Love may be the only young people's sex guide around that begins with human sexuality and ends with a discussion of the birds and the bees, but among the other topics covered en route are how to discuss sex with parents, same-sex relationships, massage, venereal disease, sex myths and birth and birth control.

Looking back over her career Dr. Hamilton realizes that she was one of the pioneers of sex counseling, a fact she credits, in part, to her Oregon childhood. "There was still a sense of the frontier when I was young, and I think because of that I grew up without thinking I was at a disadvantage because I was a girl. We were just as valued as the boys. There was a sense that you could do anything you wanted and that you would probably succeed. We were awfully innocent as children, innocent and ignorant. I can never remember sex being mentioned. An amazing number of my classmates at the University of Oregon became pregnant as undergraduates, and they didn't know what to do about it. I think that's what set me off on the road I followed." Later, she worked with her husband, A. E. Hamilton, a psychologist, received her Ph.D. at Columbia University and shared a practice with Wardell Pomeroy of the Kinsey Institute.

"What I want young people to learn," she says, "is that

it takes a lot more skill to love than to have sex, that one has to find a way to have responsible sex and be a responsible human being. Loving is when the well-being of your beloved is as essential as your own." (1978)

WILLIAM HAMILTON

"Cartooning," William Hamilton said recently, "is a way to live without working." But if Hamilton hasn't been working, he's certainly kept himself busy these last several years turning out six cartoons a week for the *San Francisco Chronicle* and several a month for *The New Yorker*.

Hamilton's characters tend to be fashionably rumpled Ivy League types. Even when they are making fools of themselves, they are "Terribly Nice People"—to use the title of his new collection of cartoons.

"Your models are yourself," Hamilton says, and in fact he looks remarkably like the sort of person who pops up in his drawings. "I was at a cocktail party the other night and somebody asked me if I knew so-and-so. I said we had been to Yale together. The man's an incredibly pompous ass, and I've used him several times in cartoons. It turned out that he was also at the party. Later we ran into each other and were in the midst of a strained conversation when the host came up with a silly grin and said, 'Ah, artist and model.' That didn't make the evening any easier."

I asked Hamilton if people were uneasy about meeting him, if they were afraid they might say something that would turn up later as a cartoon caption in *The New Yorker*. "For a lot of people it's like meeting a psychiatrist. They're very careful at first, but then they forget and become fair game. Actually, it is only rarely that you hear something you can use as is. Cartooning is a physical activity, not a mental one. It never works when you try to stage a scene. You get an idea and then play around with it and see if something happens. For instance, a couple of weeks ago I realized that I was sick and tired of trendy clothes made out of denim. So I've been making sketches of a man and a woman talking about denim. I don't know what's going to happen with it, but when I've finished it will probably look as though it's part of a conversation I've overheard somewhere."

Hamilton admits to having had a lifetime love affair with ink. "I've never liked paint or charcoal or pencil. I never sketch my drawings in pencil and then ink them. I always use ink from the very beginning, and the ink itself plays a key role in the creation of a picture." In his introduction to *Terribly Nice People*, Hamilton has written: "You can't use a pen dipped in ink the way you do an IBM typewriter. Ink is too mortal: Your pen starts out overloaded, becomes just right, and then runs out in a rhythm completely oblivious to your train of thought."

Like most younger cartoonists, Hamilton refuses to use captions written by someone else—a fairly common practice, Hamilton says, among older cartoonists. "If you use outside material you stand in great danger of becoming a parody of yourself. When you write your own lines you might get bad ones every now and then, but you are growing. You aren't cutting off your future."

Hamilton and his wife and young daughter recently moved from the East Coast to San Francisco. I wondered if that had had any effect on his work. "People are in New York to get ahead," he said. "Why else would they live there? In California there's not so much pressure for success. If you fail there, well, things just aren't as bad for you as they are in the East. But luckily for me, people in San Francisco say just as many stupid things as they do in New York. And I listen to them." (1976)

78.

SEAMUS HEANEY

eamus Heaney was born in County Derry in 1939, the year William Butler Yeats died. In the past ten years he has published four books of poems, and more often than not when you see his name in print he is described as Ireland's best living poet, sometimes as the best since Yeats himself.

Yeats, the Southern Protestant senator, and Heaney, the son of a Northern Catholic farmer, seem an ill-suited pair of poets. Heaney and I had a chance to talk about that recently. He was passing through New York City on his way home from a Yeats festival on Long Island where he read poems from *North*, his new book. "Yeats," he said, "has never had the slightest influence on my inner workings. But as I get older and begin to recognize the tension between the inner person—the poet—and the outer person—the professional, public figure—I've come to admire Yeats as a strategist. He navigated very skillfully."

Heaney has had to do some skillful navigation of his own. In 1972, after a year as a guest lecturer at the University of California ("Berkeley loosened the soil around my taproot"), he and his wife and children moved from Belfast in Northern Ireland to County Wicklow in the south.

Since the publication of his first book, *Death of a Naturalist*, Heaney had been held up as a new voice of Ireland and, he said, "people had begun to think of me as a political symptom rather than as a poet." *North* contains a poem that begins with an encounter with "an English journalist in search of 'views on the Irish thing,'" the sort of interview that had become both commonplace and bothersome for Heaney. "Even worse," he continued, "I began to lose sense of myself as a poet. Some poets find the political role an exciting one. You always have your political life on the line, but I found it more exhilarating to get out."

Part of getting out was his literal rediscovery of the soil

beneath his feet. "Years before," he said, "I had written a poem called 'Bogland,' and for some reason I began to think more and more about it. As a boy I grew up next to a bog. I'd read P. V. Glob's book about bog people, with all its photographs of perfectly preserved 2000-year-old bodies found in the bogs of Jutland. I'd seen all the marvelous things dug out of Irish bogs that they now have in the National Museum in Dublin. It seemed to me that bogs had great symbolic possibilities residing in them and not forced upon them by poetic invention. They have a memory."

He wrote in *North:* "I love this turf-face / its black incisions, / the cooped secrets / of process and ritual."

With the photographs of the ancient sacrifice victims from Glob's *The Bog People* in mind, he also began to think about Ireland's roots in northern Europe and of the Viking occupation of Dublin. "I thought," he said, "that unrest thousands of years ago in Jutland could be swirled in an Irish pot. I suppose it became an obsessive image, but I began to think of Irish nationalism as a territorial and feminine religion as old as the bogs themselves. All the people going out to kill have the religion."

The longest section of *North* begins and ends with poems about Antaeus, the giant in Greek mythology who received new strength whenever he touched the ground and who was eventually defeated by Hercules, who simply held him off the ground until he weakened. "I see it," Heaney says, "as a little parable about the myth of colonization. The colonizer has the Herculean force to raise up the native from his roots, and then to weaken him.

"When you are born in Ireland you are given a ready-made world. Someone, a Rumanian, I think, called it 'the coherent miseries of an oppressed, small place.' But it is a surface world, and it is not enough. You have to nest upon it, incubate it into something greater, to release something unusual from it. Like ancient bodies from a bog."   (1976)

A. LEON HIGGINBOTHAM, JR.

"**W**hen, in the television show *Roots*, Kunta Kinte's foot was amputated, people were shocked, but they probably didn't realize that mutilation of slaves was perfectly legal. And they didn't know that if his master had taught him to read, rather than maiming him, it would have been illegal." The speaker is A. Leon Higginbotham, Jr., United States Circuit Judge for the Third Circuit (Philadelphia), one of only six black Americans to have reached the Federal Appellate bench and a man many judicial insiders think is destined for the Supreme Court.

Judge Higginbotham, 50, has just published his first book, *In the Matter of Color*, a study of the racial laws in six of the American Colonies before the Revolution. It is the result of nearly fifteen years of research into Colonial documents. "Blacks," he said during a recent visit to New York, "had few friends in court. In researching what happened from 1619, when the first slaves arrived, to 1776, we found no handy index entry for Black Injustice in the law books. We had to read through everything, and we found material in unlikely places. Out of mortgage law, for example, we got into the legal question of whether slaves were considered 'real estate' or 'livestock.' We found long legal entries on something called 'slave insanity.' Do you know what that means? It means a slave who wanted to be free. In some Colonies blacks, but not whites, could be used for medical experimentation. In some Colonies blacks and whites could attend the same church services, but only if the preacher were a white man.

"What we seem to forget, if we ever learned it, is that there is a respectable legal basis for all the injustice done the blacks, that their special level of humiliation was rooted in law and not simply social custom."

It is ironic, Judge Higginbotham points out, that the first Emancipation Proclamation in America was not Lincoln's. In 1775 Lord Dunmore, the British governor of Virginia, offered freedom to any slave who would take the king's shilling and join the Royal Army. "Few blacks took Dunmore up on his offer, but it is interesting to think what might have happened if the British had been able to lure the slave population to its side. As for the Declaration of Independence, that great attack on man-made law, it didn't speak for the blacks. Remember what Frederick Douglass said, 'The Fourth of July is yours, not mine.'

"But there never has been, in our country, a 'proper time' for black rights. In 1776 blacks couldn't be free because there was a war to fight. After the Civil War, there was a country to be put back in shape. In 1917 there was a world war and blacks couldn't be unpatriotic. In 1941 there was another. And so on and so on until events caught up with us with the Civil Rights Acts of the 1960s, and finally it indeed became law that all men—all persons—are created equal."   (1978)

THE BROTHERS HILDEBRANDT

Greg and Tim Hildebrandt are twins in their late 30s, and they've been painting together since they were 3 years old. Literally, painting together. One will start on the left-hand side of a picture and paint toward the middle, the other will start on the right. If the picture is too small for them to work at the same time, they take turns. Afterward, they can't tell who painted what.

The Brothers Hildebrandt, as their publisher likes to call them, have made a name for themselves as fantasy painters, first with annual Tolkien calendars and now with the illustrations—including a full-color centerfold—for a novel, *The Sword of Shannara*, by Terry Brooks. The Brooks novel is a 726-page epic full of dwarfs, gnomes, elves, giant druids and an evil Warlock Lord, all battling over an enchanted landscape for control of a magic sword. Everyone involved in the project warns that one should not compare *The Sword* with Tolkien's *Lord of the Rings* ("The only thing they have in common is that they are both fantasies," says editor Judy-Lynn del Rey), but that's pretty much like telling a child to stand in the corner and not—definitely *not*—think of dragons.

Greg, who is a few hours older than Tim and seems to be the family spokesman, says flatly, "Tolkien saved our souls. When we started doing the calendars we were spared a lifetime of designing cat food boxes and drawing pandas for kids' books. And now with Brooks, things couldn't be better. We've never met him, but his fantasy is ours."

The Hildebrandts live within a few miles of each other in New Jersey, and they paint in a barn behind Greg's house. Between them, they have four children, and when it comes time to plan a picture, they dress up their wives, children, even neighbors, in medieval costumes and photograph them. "We have a whole closet full of stuff," Tim says, "capes, boots, tights, fancy sleeves. They're made so they can come apart, and we put them back together in different ways for different pictures."

Greg points out that although they photograph their amateur models, they don't trace the photographs or seek photorealism. "The paintings have to look real, but not quite. Our influences are Howard Pyle and N. C. Wyeth, of course, but also early Disney films. Like them, we want to create worlds to step into."

The brothers say that being twins has caused few problems for them. "We feed off each other," Greg says. "The rest of the world doesn't really exist. We live in fantasy, and it's how we've lived since we were kids." And in their dreams, do they dream of monsters and elves? "Never of monsters," says Greg. "We dream of mixing colors. But when we were kids we did have one dream that we shared."

Tim said, "We would dream that we went down the cellar steps of our house in Detroit, into the dark. At the bottom, we would turn around and the stairs would be gone, and then we saw eyes glowing in the dark."

"That's all," Greg said, "just eyes."

They are now finishing up the 1978 Tolkien calendar (they work in acrylics on six-feet-square sheets of gessoed Masonite) and are planning a huge mural for their publisher's office. "The question is, do we start at the door to the ladies' room and paint to the fire escape or begin at the fire escape and head for the ladies' room?" After that, they will illustrate Brooks's sequel to *The Sword of Shannara*.

"When we go into our barn," Greg says, "we slip the board across the door and go through the mirror. Our kids are often there, running around and playing. They might look at what we are painting every now and then and say, 'Oh, it's just another dragon.' It's their world, too. You see, fantasy is not an escape out of anything, it's an escape into something."

(1977)

AL HIRSCHFELD

Al Hirschfeld, the theater caricaturist, began his career almost 60 years ago as a cartoonist for the communist *New Masses* magazine. He lost that job—nonpaying, as he now recalls—when the editors rejected an unflattering drawing of Father Coughlin, the right-wing radio orator. "They sent up a committee to explain to me that they didn't want to offend Catholic trade unionists," he said the other day, "and that was the end of my political career. I've avoided committees ever since."

He has also avoided editorial comment in his drawings. "My job is to interpret a body—a whole body—in line and make it clear to the reader what is going on. I don't think making a big nose bigger is funny, and I don't like drawings of big heads and little bodies. The way a person stands or sits or walks—or dances —is important. You've got to show it all, and if my drawing doesn't really look like the person, well, I've found that readers begin to think the person looks like my drawing. I used to love to draw Ray Bolger. Any chance I got I drew him—the way his fingers curled when he danced, everything. One day I told him that, and you know what he told me? He said he saved all my drawings of him and copied them when he danced. All those years we were just copying each other."

Hirschfeld was sitting in an old barber's chair on the top floor of his Eastside Manhattan brownstone. In front of him was his drawing board. I had dropped by to talk with him about his new book, *Hirschfeld*, a collection of 200 or so recent drawings.

Outside, carved over the bay window on the second floor was a bearded head—not, however, Hirschfeld's. "When Dolly and I first saw this place 32 years ago," he says, "I saw that beard and thought it was a good omen. We bought the house and I've been sitting here ever since. Now a committee of five psychiatrists keeps trying to buy the place for any amount I'll name. It must be a good neighborhood for *meshugenahs*."

Most of the sketches in the new book—which range from Mikhail Baryshnikov to Lily Tomlin to Warren Beatty to the Smothers Brothers—come from *The New York Times*, where Hirschfeld drawings have been appearing since 1925. "I go to rehearsals and work away in the dark," he says. "I've trained myself so I can even sketch with my hand in my pocket. The sketches would look to you like a lot of hieroglyphics, but I can read them when I get back to my drawing board. I watch the performers move, but I can't pay any attention to what's going on. If I did, I'd end up with an empty sketch pad. I just got back from out of town, where I saw the new Tom Stoppard play and spent a good deal of time sketching the male lead. Now I've learned that he's been replaced. I have a mass of sketches, but I don't remember if he was good or bad. I always go on opening night to find out—*pour le sport*."   (1980)

ANNE HOLLANDER

"**C**lothes aren't something we put over our true selves," says Anne Hollander. "Clothes are our true selves. In fact, we see nudity in terms of the clothes that aren't there." Miss Hollander, an art historian, has recently published a book, *Seeing Through Clothes*, which traces the ways artists have seen clothing—and the bodies underneath—from the days of the classical Greeks to the present.

"Officially dress is considered frivolous," she continues, "something linked to the baser side of man. It is no accident that in Titian's allegorical *Sacred and Profane Love* the figure who represents the profane is the one who is wearing the clothes." Anne Hollander has large brown eyes and an unusually expressive face. It was worth the price of lunch just to see her facial impressions of Titian's symbolic women. Before we hit dessert she had mimed a classical Venus, several versions of the Virgin Mary and one of Ingres's 19th-century matrons. I suspect she could sum up Picasso's *Guernica* with a flared nostril and one raised eyebrow.

"Dress, of course, is ephemeral," she goes on to say, "but it is preserved in art, and since the 15th century pictures have dictated the way people dress. I have become a crank on this subject. Today dress is conceived in terms of the camera. In the past painters may have left out the clavicle when they did portraits, but cameras show clavicles, and dresses are now designed to show—or hide—them. We are committed to pictures because they tell us what to look for. They are sacred to us. Even when we look in the mirror we are making our own pictures, and they are less truthful than snapshots."

Before the invention of the camera people still had pictures to dress by. "Since the 15th century there have been pop graphics," Miss Hollander says. "At any fair, for the price of a penny you could get a picture of a saint or the Virgin or

Jesus. There would be Jesus in his Jesus suit. No one would dress like that. But off to one side would be the duke, in his duke suit, praying away. You might like to dress like that if you had the money. And maybe scattered around in the background are people dressed the way you and your neighbors know is the way to dress.

"It is a hoax to think of the influence of art in terms of its greatest works. The influence of first-rate art is not all that far from third-rate. What is erotic in Michelangelo is just as erotic in *Penthouse*. We become excited, nervous, scared, sexed-up. That's what art does, and it also tells us what we think we look like."

(1979)

CHRISTOPHER ISHERWOOD

Christopher Isherwood, author of the Berlin novels that became the basis for *I Am a Camera* and *Cabaret*, has, at age 72, decided to stop playing the pronoun game. In his dozen or so volumes of fiction and autobiography, it is rarely clear whom his hero "Christopher" is sleeping with, although few readers would assume when Christopher says "Love had been J. for the last month" that "J." stands for Jennie or Jessica. Now in *Christopher and His Kind*, an autobiography that covers 1929 to 1939, chiefly the Berlin years, Isherwood makes it all perfectly clear. "To Christopher," he writes, "Berlin meant Boys."

Isherwood, who has lived in Southern California since the early 1940s, visited New York recently and we talked about his new book. "It began as a preface to my American diaries, which I'll be publishing soon. As I was editing them and adding new comments, it became obvious that I needed some sort of explanation for what I was doing over here in the first place. That began a chain of events that led back to my leaving Britain for Berlin in 1929. I realized that once I left home for Germany, going to America was inevitable, and the preface turned into a book. I didn't say to myself: now's the time to tear off the mask. I just decided that if I were going to tell the story I'd tell it all. In the earlier books Christopher was really quite a faceless young man. The reader only saw what he saw. This time I've tried to make him a character and not an observer."

By using the phrase "I am a camera" in *Goodbye to Berlin*, Isherwood gave book reviewers a line they've never forgotten, but he now says the camera-eye technique of writing is "a sort of flirtation with the reader that I rather dislike." He continues, "Just as in the classic detective story, you shouldn't cheat. The clues are all there if you look, but you have to piece them together. There was a real clash in my mind between the joy of weaving plots and the realization that for me writing was not the rendition of a story but the rendition of life. Other writers are more interested in the interplay of characters, and I am more interested in the feel of them. Jack Kerouac is a writer I enjoy. Nothing much really happens in his books. No one gets murdered, but every-thing happens. You get life. Before Tolstoy wrote *War and Peace*, he wrote a novel about simply what happened during one day. I've never been able to locate a copy, but I would rather read it than what came next."

Although Isherwood says that the Christopher of the Berlin years is now "a person I no longer completely under-stand," he doesn't accuse him of being overcautious as a writer. "Avoiding the homosexual issue wasn't a matter of caution. One just didn't want to open that can of beans. There were too many beans for that. What I was really writing would have been swamped. I had my grievances, but if I dwelt on them I would have become a bore. Anyway, I assumed people could read me. It's possible to spot homosexual writing just as it is possible to spot Jewish writing."

Our talk turned to Christopher's father, Lieutenant Colonel Frank Isherwood, who with thousands of other British soldiers was lost in the mud and confusion of Ypres in World War I. "He knitted in the trenches, long scarves and that sort of thing. I'm sure that made him the butt of jokes among the men. But I think it was his way of getting his men out of a state of panic. The greatest quality of true heroes is that they reassure others and make them brave." I suspect that *Christopher and His Kind* is Isherwood's own version of knitting in the trenches. "I feel a stronger alliance to my group than to any nation," he had said earlier in the interview. "I take pains not to defend myself on this subject, but I never thought of myself as being part of England. I'd sooner fight in defense of homosexuality than of any nation." (1977)

ANNE JACKSON

Anne Jackson was born just up the Allegheny River from Pittsburgh, the youngest daughter of a gloomy Irish Catholic mother and an energetic Croatian socialist father, who, given a chance, introduced himself as Citizen John Jackson. The Jacksons moved to Brooklyn when Anne was 8, but she never forgot that Pennsylvania river valley. "I still can't remember whether Pittsburgh ends with a 'g' or an 'h,'" she said the other day, "but I can remember Job's Hole, where we lived, as being as beautiful as Portofino." She was sitting in the sunny, book-cluttered living room of the Manhattan apartment she shares with her husband, Eli Wallach, talking about her new book, *Early Stages*.

"I worked on the book off and on for four years and

whenever someone heard that it was memoirs of my childhood they wanted to know at what age I'd stop. I never had an answer for them. When does childhood end, if ever? The one thing I've learned in the theater is not to play the ending until you get there. When I was going to do Saint Joan I was terrified. How could I play a martyr? But then I realized that martyrs, like everyone else, don't know how their stories will end. They just keep going until they pass the point of no return, when they say, 'I'd rather die than give up now.' Holy martyrdom," she added with a laugh, "that's my approach to writing."

She originally began by talking her story into a tape recorder, but that didn't work. "I started acting out all the parts in dialect, especially my father's, and I became aware of an unseen audience. I began to show off. Again it was like the theater. If you become aware of the audience and play to it, you begin to get fancy and you get into trouble. My father, just before he died, began writing his autobiography. He called it *Joy of Finding*, and it began, 'It's writer's profound wish to depict, without any flowering, truth as it happened.' I decided to follow his example."

Early Stages follows the Jacksons from western Pennsylvania, where Anne spotted "little men" dancing under an oak tree ("It's a sure sign of rain," said Great-Aunt Nell Judy), through the sadder years in Brooklyn, when Anne's mother was confined to a mental hospital, to Anne's first Off Broadway roles and her marriage to Eli Wallach.

As if on cue, Wallach came into the living room with a copy of the morning's *Daily News*. One of the columnists had praised *Early Stages* by saying it was a relief to read an actress' autobiography that didn't reveal a love affair with a Kennedy. "That's unfair," said Anne, "I never had one.

"The thing that has most surprised me, though, is the effect the book has had on the children. The other day Eli was in a dither about something and one of our daughters, who had just read the book, said, 'Don't yell at Mommy. She had a terrible childhood.' It wasn't a terrible childhood, but I think it was the first time she realized that I even had one."

(1979)

JULIAN JAYNES

Early in the year, Julian Jaynes published a book and just about no one noticed. It has a plain black-and-white dust jacket; its binding is textbook blue and gold; and its title is *The Origin of Consciousness in the Breakdown of the Bicameral Mind.* Slowly, reviewers around the country have started to take notice of it and are turning out long reviews that usually end with the comment that whether or not Jaynes is correct, what he has to say is provocative.

What he has to say is that man was not a conscious being until about 1000 B.C. Before then he operated in an unconscious state, directed by inner "voices" that were probably taken to be divine. The voices, Jaynes believes, were simply the right side of the brain giving orders to the left. Jaynes, 55 years old, with a Ph.D. from Yale, is a maverick psychology instructor and researcher at Princeton. He said the other day that readers who are impressed with his book are classicists (it contains a long study of language in the *Iliad,* showing the epic poem to be the work of unconscious minds and later amended by conscious ones) and historians. As for his psychologist colleagues: "They hate it," he says, "which hardly surprises me. There's no science so tied to fashion as psychology. It's worse than the New York garment industry, and the fashion these days is behaviorism. What I'm saying is that behaviorism would have been a useful study until man became conscious. Now it is useless."

Jaynes has been at work on *The Origin of Consciousness* for almost thirty years. To talk with him, even for a few minutes, is to realize that he has pursued the evolution of consciousness with amazing single-mindedness. But he would add that "evolution" is precisely the wrong word to use in reference to consciousness. "Consciousness is learned," he says, "it did not generate like a flower. But once learned it is highly contagious. Like arithmetic. Think how many hundreds of generations it took to come up with the idea of zero. Now any child can grasp it. Just by saying, 'Johnny, stop and think,' a parent teaches consciousness. By 5 or 6 most children are conscious."

Jaynes warns that one should not underestimate the unconscious mind. "So much of what we think of as consciousness, isn't. You can learn by unconscious imitation. Because we are conscious, when we do anything new we are very aware of it, but that probably hinders our learning ability, especially when it comes to physical things such as bike riding, or dancing, or hitting a nail with a hammer. The unconscious man wasn't uncreative. Just look at the Mayas, the ancient Greeks, the people of Mesopotamia."

But sometime before 1000 B.C. the world became too complex for the bicameral mind and its voices. Man began to write and use metaphors. He taught himself to be conscious and with consciousness came a sense of time. The voices became silent. "Achilles," says Jaynes, "didn't have a sense of living a lifetime. We do. He didn't think of having been born, of growing old and of dying. We have the advantages of memory and imagination, and I think memory is largely imagination. The ability to look back is not all that different from the ability to look ahead." But man also came to miss the sound of the inner voices and long for them, which, Jaynes suggests, accounts for the birth of religion. "Because we have memory," he says, "we also have guilt, and the only way to dissipate guilt is forgiveness, which is what our religions are based on."

Jaynes says he once heard a voice which, he thinks, might have been a vestige of his old bicameral voice. When he was in his 20s, already at work on the origins of consciousness, he heard one day a voice in the right side of his brain say, "Include the knower in the known." Years later, lecturing on his bicameral theory at Cornell, he told of the incident and someone in the back of the hall shouted out, "You should have paid attention to that and not gone on with this."

"Well, I went on with it," Jaynes says. "I've gone beyond evidence in my book, and I'm out on a limb waiting to be disproved. So far, I'm still waiting." (1977)

92.

JUNE JORDAN

When a poet wins a Prix de Rome and is invited to spend a year at the American Academy in Rome, the usual assumption is that poetry has something to do with the award. In the case of June Jordan—who has more than a half-dozen poetry collections to her credit and whose *Things That I Do in the Dark* (selected poems) has just been published—the assumption would be wrong. She won a Prix de Rome in 1970 for environmental design, and it was awarded not for her poetry or even for a nonfiction study of the environment but for a novel, *His Own Where.*

The book is set in her former Bedford-Stuyvesant neighborhood in Brooklyn, and it was written entirely in black English. "I had used black dialect in my poetry," she said recently, "but I wanted to show that you could also use it for description, for moving the plot along, everything. I wanted to show just how flexible black English is." She describes the novel as "a primer on urban neighborhoods" that shows how the people themselves can rebuild a slum without spending any money. "Or at least not much money," she adds. "It was largely a matter of changing attitudes, of pride."

Buckminster Fuller read the book, liked it and sponsored her for the Prix de Rome. She and Fuller had met a few years earlier. "I used to hang out in the architecture section of the New York Public Library," she says. "It was a nice, quiet place to write. When I wasn't working I'd browse around, and that's how I came across Bucky Fuller's books. *Esquire* magazine had been wanting me to write something for them, and about the same time—this was in 1968—there had been some bad rioting in Harlem. I'd been born there and lived there until my parents moved to Brooklyn. I happened to be up there while the riots were going on, and they radicalized me. I began to have racist feelings toward whites, and for the sake of my sanity I wanted to stop that. I wanted to fight back without fighting and began to wonder what

Harlem would look like if Fuller and I redesigned the place. I suggested it to *Esquire*, and they got the two of us together. It was a saving experience."

The result of the Fuller-Jordan partnership ran in the magazine under the title "Instant Slum Clearance." The eye-catching thing about the plan is that new buildings were built above existing ones, so that the neighborhoods would not be destroyed while they were being rebuilt. Later, the original buildings would be replaced or renovated. "Things actually got out of hand," Miss Jordan says with a smile. "By the time we finished I think Bucky had those buildings a hundred stories tall."

But June Jordan still thinks of herself as a poet. "I'm a poet automatically and unconsciously. I never think of myself as anything but a poet. My father force-fed me to read, really force-fed: the Bible, Shakespeare, Dunbar, Poe. I liked the sounds of words before I understood what they meant. I wrote my first poem when I was 9, about Flag Day I think. It went so well I started writing poems on demand, especially for kids in love. I picked up a lot of change that way."

In putting together *Things That I Do in the Dark*, she arranged her poems not chronologically (although the date for each poem is given) but by theme: love poems, poems about the black experience, travel poems, protest poems. "Putting it together," she says, "was like looking at myself for the first time. My son was a baby when I wrote the earliest ones, and now he's a Harvard sophomore. I was surprised to find that I'd been writing about South Africa as early as 1960. I had forgotten that. As for the love poems, I was surprised how understated the early ones were, as though I were afraid to let the reader in. Now I'm less fearful. I move over and give the reader some room."

As for the title *Things That I Do in the Dark*, "That's literally true. I wait up until everyone's asleep and then I go to work on my poems." (1978)

THOMAS KENEALLY

A few months ago the London *Times Literary Supplement* ran a letter to the editor that ended with an apology. It was signed by Thomas Keneally, the Australian novelist whose books include *A Dutiful Daughter* and *Blood Red, Sister Rose*, and in it he discussed his new novel, *Gossip from the Forest*. The book deals with the November, 1918, armistice negotiations that were held in a dining car parked on a railway siding in the forest at Compiègne, France. "The characters," he wrote in the letter, "of Erzberger, Foch, Weygand and others are extensively researched." But there was one man on the scene, a German count, whom he could find little about. So he created a personality to fill the gap. Keneally added that "by creating fictions about men from the past a writer can cause pain to living relatives" and then went on to apologize.

The return address on the letter was a small town in suburban Connecticut, and I contacted Keneally to talk about the novel and the apology. "As for the count," he said, "I just assumed that none of his family could have survived the Nazis, so I attributed to him some horror stories I'd been wanting to use for years. We've changed his name in the American edition." This is not the first time Keneally has fleshed out historical figures. He says that in *Blood Red, Sister Rose* Joan of Arc's tormentors are based on various Australian politicians and that he modeled Joan herself on Germaine Greer, a fellow Australian. "I wanted a gutsy, foul-mouthed girl, and where are you going to find girls like that today except in New York City or Australia?"

Keneally became interested in the 1918 armistice negotiations after a producer asked him to write a filmscript about the last day of World War I. In the course of doing some background research he came across the name of Matthias Erzberger, a governmental official who headed the German delegation at the talks. He promptly gave up the filmscript and went to work on Erzberger. "The losing side obviously sends the least argumentative spokesmen, but Erzberger kept exact records of everything he did, and his wanderings from one governmental office to another looking for instructions read like Joseph K.'s in *The Trial*. Germany was on the brink of socialist revolution. The whole history of Europe could have been changed in a few days. It was a fascinating time."

The villains of the novel, though, are the French. "I'm intensely anti-French," Keneally admits. "I see Foch's behavior as just a prelude to the kind of French arrogance we've been seeing ever since. He was an ignorant, closed-minded bigot, and in World War I he and other French generals used Australians as cannon fodder while they hid behind the lines. Did you notice the dedication of *Gossip from the Forest*? It reads, 'In the season in which this book was written, the French government persisted in exploding nuclear devices above the ocean where my children swim.' The simple bloody truth is that these bastards were setting off bombs just off Australia. It would be just the same for you if they were dropping A-bombs off Cape Cod."

I asked him how long he and his family planned to stay in Connecticut. "We're here for less than a year. One reason I came over was that I thought the Australian critics were going to kill me for *Gossip*, but they loved it. One critic wrote that he felt he shouldn't like it because it wasn't sufficiently Australian, but then he decided it was time to get over that sort of nationalism. Back there, we're at the age the U.S. was in the 1890s. It's just now becoming a fit place for writers and artists. Middle-aged writers are still at work with the London critics in mind, but the younger ones write for Australians. Being a cultural colony takes a lot longer to get over than being a political colony. Americans should know that. Canadians know it even more so.

"I think Canada is even less culturally self-confident than Australia. Canadians have been dominated by both the U.S. and England. At least we're nicely far away and buffered by Oriental societies. I don't think most people realize how strong an influence the Orient plays on Australian culture.

Jakarta Indonesian is the most popular foreign language taught in the schools.

"Most Australians, though, grow up thinking that they are only half Australian, that they have another half in some mysterious place called Back Home, which usually means England or Ireland. That's why Australians are always traveling. The shock is to find that your whole self has really been Australian all the time, the way you tell a joke or drink booze, anything. Everything."

(1976)

ROBERT F. KENNEDY, JR.

In October, 1975, Robert F. Kennedy, Jr., drove down to Alabama to do research for his senior thesis at Harvard. His subject was to be Governor George Wallace, and the length of the paper was not to exceed forty pages. He ended up staying in Alabama for eight months, and when he finished writing he had a 300-page manuscript dealing not with the governor but with Judge Frank M. Johnson, Jr., Wallace's former law-school friend, who became his bitterest local enemy in the legal battles over integration.

Kennedy is now bringing the thesis out in book form (*Judge Frank M. Johnson, Jr.*), and he talked about it recently in his publisher's office in New York. "When I got to Alabama, Governor Wallace couldn't have been any nicer to me. He said he would give me all the help he could and I think he meant it, but I found that the real power down there was in the hands of this federal judge from the hill country up in the north-central part of the state. His name was Frank Johnson, and he had reluctantly taken over just about every functioning institution in the state. He was running everything. He was the man who integrated, or ordered integrated, the schools, buses and libraries. He ruled against the poll tax and the Klan. He even reformed the mental hospitals and prisons. If Judge Johnson has his way, the most progressive prison reform in the country will be coming out of one of the least progressive states."

Judge Johnson was later President Carter's first choice for the head of the FBI, but he had to decline because of ill health. "He's feeling all right now," Kennedy says, "but I think it's just as well that he didn't become director. As the FBI is now set up, that's a dead-end job, and I don't think he would have liked being a little fish in a big pond like Washington. And he does like being a big fish in Montgomery. I'd been told, before I met him, that he was a scary, serious, distant man, but the real Johnson is an approachable hillbilly. He's out of a family of old-style Lincoln Republicans who refused to fight on the side of the Confederacy. They've been isolated up in those hills for years. They believe in law and the Constitution, and they are free of racism."

Kennedy did no writing in Alabama (he saved that for Massachusetts and his grandmother Rose's home in Florida), but he talked a lot and took notes. "I find it hard to sit still during the day," he says, "but I interviewed a couple of hundred people: friends, enemies, politicians, law clerks, just plain old racists. I always told them who I was and what I was doing. I think people talked a lot more openly with me than they would for regular reporters. I think they sensed that I would respect their privacy because I've had enough trouble with that subject myself."

And he also spent a good deal of time with Judge Johnson. "He taught me how to fish for sea trout out of a little rented dinghy in the Gulf. The only fishing I'd ever done was trolling off the back of a motorboat. I had never realized that fishing involved skill. The sea trout always does the same thing. It grabs the shrimp bait by the tail and runs with it.

Then it drops the shrimp and turns and bites it on the head. You have to pull right then or you'll lose the fish, but you can't pull too hard because they have weak lower jaws."

Kennedy is currently editing, for a British publisher, a college-level anthology of historians discussing their craft. He's working on the book at the home of a friend in Lowndes County (called "Bloody Lowndes" during the days of the freedom rides and marches), Alabama.

"It's a great place to get things done," he says, although he has no plans to live there permanently. "I'm a New Yorker," he says, "with an apartment here in the city." I mentioned to him a very funny street-corner speech I once heard his father give in Brooklyn, a parody of the carpetbagger speeches used against him when he was running for the Senate. "The real carpetbaggers," said Kennedy, "were my uncles who ran for office in Massachusetts. Except for summers on Cape Cod, they were all brought up in Bronxville. No, we're New Yorkers. I love it here. It's alive."   (1978)

JERZY KOSINSKI

In *Blind Date*, Jerzy Kosinski's new novel, the central character, Levanter, misses being at Sharon Tate's Hollywood Hills home on the night of the Manson gang murders because of an airline mix-up. Kosinski himself missed being at the Tate home that night because a French airline clerk sent his luggage to New York rather than to Los Angeles.

That missed appointment in Hollywood is only one of

many examples of chance at work in the novel. Other random encounters lead to murder, practical jokes, rape, escape from behind the Iron Curtain, incest, even a happy marriage. The book, in fact, is made up almost entirely of chance incidents and blind dates. "There should be no promise of plot," Kosinski said the other day in his New York apartment. "That would be a fraud. Plot is extraordinary, while chance is ordinary." The apartment is large and sunny, with many plants and framed photographs. A huge bear trap hangs on one wall. On the terrace is a garden hose, and Kosinski, like Levanter in *Blind Date*, sometimes amuses himself by squirting it at pedestrians entering the subway station on the street corner eighteen stories below.

"Many people," Kosinski says, "miss out on life itself because they believe that life has a plot. We are trained very early to believe that life has a plan and we have only to find it. Parents are always telling their children, 'One day you'll find out.' That is nonsense. Life is a series of incidents, and if we don't train ourselves to perceive the individual moments we won't understand our lives."

Kosinski says his account of the Manson killings in *Blind Date*, told from the point of view of his murdered friend, Woytek Frykowski, is the first time the story has not been told from the murderers' viewpoint. "There is a reason why people have focused on the killers," he says. "People don't want to believe they, too, could be victims of a pointless attack. People want to believe that they are safe from chance and that their homes are fortresses."

Kosinski believes his own life is something of a testament to chance. He was born in the Polish Ukraine in 1933, and when the Nazis invaded the country his parents sent him off alone to escape eastward. His journey through Poland became the basis of his first novel, *The Painted Bird* (1965). After the war he studied in Poland and Russia. "My interest was photographic chemicals, a subject the government had little interest in." During the famous Khrushchev "thaw" he won a passport to the United States by claiming he had a fellowship to study there. He hadn't, but he taught himself English (he writes, now, only in English), worked as a parking-lot attendant and later studied political science at Columbia University.

He also discovered that he wanted to write. His first two books, published under a pseudonym, were nonfiction studies of Soviet life. An admirer of one of them was the widow of a steel tycoon, who sent Kosinski a fan letter. The two met, although he was under the impression he was meeting the woman's secretary. "She seemed far too young to be the widow of a man I knew to be very old when he died, so we went off to dinner without my ever knowing who she was." Later they married and lived together until her death in 1968. Levanter finds his wife in a similar way in *Blind Date*.

"So far," Kosinski says, "I've written six novels, and they've all been didactic. I'm not writing popular fiction that tells a story. People ride the subways every day in a daze. They never realize the possibilities of the incidents that are going on all around them. And when they read about a subway, what do they read? *The Taking of Pelham One Two Three*. They are entertained perhaps, but they are still in a daze. That's popular fiction for you. Pop culture has all the tanks and bombers, if you want to speak of this militarily. I like to think of myself as a guerrilla fighter. The urban guerrilla has much more realistic contact with the people than the regular soldier who is kept off in an army camp somewhere in the country. And for my generation, the greatest disasters are caused by the regular soldiers. A character in my last novel, *Cockpit*, calls himself a one-man army. I am comfortable with that description of myself." (1978)

JILL KREMENTZ and THOMAS VICTOR

You pick up a new book, glance at the jacket and maybe even read a bit of what the publisher has to say on the front flap; then you flip the book over and take a look at the photograph on the back to see what the author looks like. Maybe you even take a peek at the author first thing. I wonder how much those photographs affect a reader's first impression of a book.

Too many pictures tell nothing at all. There is, for instance, the standard shot of a university-connected writer: he is wearing tweeds (leather patches on the elbows optional); there is a bookshelf in the background and usually a pipe in hand. The subject's eyes are a bit squinty as he looks with concern at the photographer, who usually turns out to be his teenage son or the English department secretary using a borrowed camera. Then there are the women of a certain age who write gothics, and their pictures—with a great deal of arty backlighting and marks of the retoucher's brush about the eyes—look as though they were taken by aging gentlemen who specialized in bridal photographs in the 1930s.

But in the last five years or so there has been a change in the art of photographing authors, a movement toward informal pictures, looking deceptively simple, of authors at ease, photographed with natural light and obviously not in a photographer's studio. Jill Krementz was one of the first exponents of this new naturalism, and I recently visited her in her light and airy—and pleasantly unfurnished—house on the East Side of Manhattan.

Although she has taken photographs since she was a little girl (she still has a meticulously arranged album of pictures— each labeled and accompanied by its negative—she took and assembled when she was about 10 years old), she did not begin taking photography seriously until she went to work as a reporter on *Show* magazine in 1961. Then came a stint as a staff photographer on the old *Herald Tribune* and five years as a reporter at *Time*. In the '60s she published two books of documentary photographs: *The Face of Vietnam*, composed of pictures taken during a year she spent in Indochina, and *Sweet Pea*, a picture book for young people, about a black girl growing up in the rural South.

"I still think of myself as a documentary photographer," she says. "My approach is documentary. I go to the subjects' houses to get them in their own settings. Background things such as chairs and pictures on the wall tell a lot about the person. They reflect the subject's style and taste. I find it distracting to photograph people in borrowed places. I have to move too much furniture to keep out all the things that just don't belong."

Indeed, some of Miss Krementz' best photographs are not the closeup shots which publishers usually choose to put on book jackets but pictures of writers in their natural habitat: Katherine Anne Porter in a lavish negligee tucked into a bed piled high with books and papers and with a crucifix tied to the headboard; Robert Penn Warren, wearing a showercap, taking a dip in a pool; Eudora Welty, in a painfully neat bedroom, framed in profile at the window like a Roman bust while in the foreground her bed lies unmade.

Miss Krementz says her career as a photographer of writers began quite by accident. At first she just took pictures of her friends, and most of her friends happened to be writers. They began to use her photographs on their book jackets, and that led to assignments. She works very quickly ("Fifteen minutes does it, if we both concentrate"), and she says she feels a moral commitment to the people she photographs. She will not release a picture for publication that has not been approved by the subject.

The image she wants to capture, she says, is the subject's own image of what he or she looks like.

A newer photographer on the literary scene is Thomas Victor, who has specialized in taking pictures of poets, perhaps because he has been a poet himself and says he finds them easy to communicate with. A few years ago he was an editor on *The New York Quarterly*, a literary magazine that didn't have enough money in its budget to afford a photographer. So Victor borrowed a friend's Nikon and started shooting away. Victor says the rules he follows as a portrait photographer are (1) to let the subjects know he is no threat; (2) to show the subjects he is interested in their work and in them; and (3) to have no preconceived ideas of the kind of picture he wants to take.

I had a chance recently to watch him photograph a writer in an office across the street from the United Nations buildings. At work, he moved like a prowler with a modified Groucho Marx lope. He never tried to be unobtrusive, and at times he got so close to his subject that he reminded me of an ophthalmologist searching for signs of glaucoma. Throughout, he kept up an odd patter ("How do you think you really look?" "Which do you like best, your wife or your work?"), but for some reason all of this—which might be expected to turn a subject into a nervous wreck—worked. Although Victor and the writer had not previously met, there was an obvious sense of growing candor and relaxation as the session continued. After about twenty minutes it was all over.

I didn't get a chance to see the pictures that came out of the session, but I would guess that the one Victor was after was not the subject's idea of what he looks like but a reflection of the nervous tension between what he actually looks like and what he would prefer to look like. That, at least, is a quality that comes through in a number of Victor photographs.

What then has caused this movement away from standard studio portraits? Jill Krementz says, "Writers have become the stars of the 1970s. People have never been so interested in writers—what they look like and how they live." The new photographic naturalism probably helps satisfy to some extent that interest while avoiding the amateurism of a candid camera. (1974)

JAMES LAUGHLIN

In 1935 James Laughlin turned his back on the family steel business in Pittsburgh and on Harvard, where he was an undergraduate, and went to France. At first he wrote press releases for Gertrude Stein, but soon he joined up with Ezra Pound in Rapallo and became a member of what Pound called his "Ezuversity." That involved running errands for Pound, playing tennis with him and, probably most important of all, keeping quiet and listening to his opinions on everything from social credit economics to medieval French poetry.

"Pound was a born teacher," Laughlin recalled recently, "but it didn't take him long to decide that I'd never be much of a writer and he told me to go back home and 'do something useful,' by which he meant become a publisher." With Pound's help Laughlin got a job editing a literary page, called "New Directions in Prose and Poetry," in a small magazine, and in 1936 he published an anthology using the same title. *New Directions 1* was a clumsy soft-bound volume, without page numbers, printed by a small press in New Hampshire. Only 600 copies in all were printed (and not all of them were sold), but the table of contents included such names as Ezra Pound, E. E. Cummings and William Carlos Williams. There were a few translations and contributions by unknown writers.

That was the beginning of New Directions Publishing Corporation, whose list over the years has included books by Pound, of course, and the Williamses (Tennessee and William Carlos), Dylan Thomas, Ferlinghetti (their best-selling poet), Djuna Barnes, Carson McCullers, Patchen, Lorca, Nabokov and James Purdy. This year marks the publication of *New Directions 30*, an anthology which, if a bit tidier than *ND 1*, is an obvious descendant.

"Our emphasis," Laughlin says, "has always been on the avant-garde, if that phrase still means anything. The annual anthology is a gallery for writers who are doing something different. We would never publish 'straight' writing. As it is we have to reject so much good stuff because of lack of space that it's painful."

Laughlin is proud of the men who have advised him on *New Directions* over the years. "I've always been open to suggestions," he says. After Pound became angry when Laughlin wouldn't publish all his friends and Yvor Winters became miffed when Laughlin wouldn't publish all his students, Laughlin was advised by Delmore Schwartz and Kenneth Rexroth.

Still, it is Pound whom Laughlin continually refers to in conversation. One of the last times he ever saw Pound was when the two of them received honorary degrees from Hamilton College in 1969. After the ceremony, at which Pound was warmly cheered by the students, they stopped at a Howard Johnson's for dinner. In the parking lot Pound balked. "Why don't you," he said, and this was during those last years when he rarely spoke, "discard me here?"　　　　(1975)

EDNA LEWIS

On a map of Virginia, Freetown in Orange County is listed as a ruin. "There's only a chimney and a few foundations, that's all," says Edna Lewis, "but we still go back for visits, it's so beautiful." Freetown was founded by her grandparents and two other families of freed slaves. Her grandfather had been a coachman, her grandmother a brick mason. They hoped their little settlement would attract other freedmen, and for a time it did. Edna Lewis grew up there and left almost forty years ago, when she was 19. She remembers it as "a lively place, with poetry readings, singing quartets and productions of plays put on by the young people."

She also remembers the food and has written a cookbook, *The Taste of Country Cooking*, to preserve the old recipes. "My brothers and sisters and I are the last of the original families—and there are no children—so I wanted to get everything down before it was lost. So much of what we shared seemed to center around food, either planting it or harvesting it or eating it. The young people have moved away and learned to eat TV dinners. Last summer when I was back in Virginia I found that people were eating a lot of cake-mix cakes and Kentucky Fried Chicken."

Her book is more than an ample collection of recipes for ham and sweet potato breakfasts or sautéed veal kidneys or plum wine or fresh peach cobbler with nutmeg sauce. It is also a record of life in Freetown, of Revival Week and Race Day, wheat threshing in July and hog slaughtering in the fall (the children saved the bladders to dry and blow up like balloons for Christmas decorations).

The recipes in *The Taste of Country Cooking* are often neither fast nor simple. "Cooking," she says, "was weaved into the way you worked. There were always lots of hands to share the work. You cooked what was growing and you arranged what you were cooking to what other chores you had. If you had to do a lot of work outside, then you'd cook something that could simmer all day on the back of the stove. We didn't eat okra, that wasn't a local crop; and black-eyed peas were a green cover crop, we never had to plant them. We were close enough to the sea to get oysters, and we always had them for Christmas. Someone would drive the thirty miles or so over to Fredericksburg to get them, and we had lots of shad in the spring. That was about the only fish we ate. Since we killed hogs only in the fall, that's when we would have pork. We sold the pigs' feet to the meatpackers and didn't pickle them. We never had ham hocks or pork chops, since we ground the meat up to make sausage. A few years ago, when people first started to use the expression, my sister asked me what 'soul food' was. I told her I didn't think it was what we used to eat."

Planting at Freetown was done on a lunar cycle. "We planted sweet potatoes and root crops during the dark of the moon, and vegetables that grew on the top of the ground in the light of the moon. There was a saying that if you planted watermelon during the dark the blossoms would fall off. Also, we planted white potatoes on St. Patrick's Day, but I don't think that had anything to do with the moon. I think it was because we called them Irish potatoes."

For the past five years Edna Lewis has been lecturing on African life to schoolchildren at the American Museum of Natural History in New York. "I try to work in cooking demonstrations as well. The children always enjoy that. And they are always surprised that when I was young I knew people who had been slaves. They seem to find it hard to believe that there was a different world than the one they know. It must seem to them like a long time ago." (1976)

JOHN LINDSAY

Mussolini wrote one novel. Disraeli turned out more than a dozen, but until now fiction—admitted fiction, that is—is something political figures on this side of the Atlantic have avoided. Now, suddenly, there are pol-made novels everywhere. Spiro Agnew has a novel. John Lindsay has a novel. William Buckley—who was once defeated by Lindsay—has a novel. John Ehrlichman has a novel. Even former New Orleans D.A. James Garrison has a novel.

John Lindsay—whose novel is entitled *The Edge*—now divides his time between being an ABC newsman and his private law practice. I dropped by his Rockefeller Center law office the other day to talk with him about his new career as a novelist. It is a corner office with an impressive view of the steeples of St. Patrick's Cathedral, and it is crowded with mementos of his seventeen years as a congressman and mayor: testimonial plaques, medals, honorary degrees, informal family pictures, a fireman's helmet, a London bobby's hat, two photographs of Winston Churchill and something that closely resembles a slot machine. Lindsay, perhaps a little grayer now, looks much as he did when his face used to peer out at us almost daily from the front page of *The New York Times.*

Before I could ask him a question, he asked me one: "What did you think of the book's ending?" I told him that I found it easier to believe the pessimism of the first half of the novel than the optimism of the second half, that finding local and national government in shreds was easier to believe than the hope that a lone congressman could almost single-handedly turn things around. It wasn't an answer that pleased him. "The upbeat ending is very important. It is very important for people to believe that there *is* hope for good government and that individuals *can* make things happen."

What made him turn to fiction? "Now that I'm a lawyer again, I spend a lot of time on planes—I've recently been to the Middle East six times on business—so I began using the time writing. I wrote a long essay about the relationship between politicians and police systems, and when I finished I realized that there are only about eight people around who would give a damn about reading it. I really wanted to say something about the process of law, the rule of law, and the absolute need for an attorney general who can say no to a president. And I thought, why not do it in a way that might be fun to read?

"When I was mayor and Johnny Carson was doing the *Tonight* show out of New York, I used to drop in every now and then. I'd usually be on for about five minutes and out of that time Carson would give me about thirty seconds to get my message across. The rest of the time was banter, but those thirty seconds were worth more than a fifteen-minute speech. I think I was trying to do pretty much the same thing with the novel."

Does he entertain any thoughts about getting back into politics? "I ran for things for seventeen years, and I have no desire to do it again. I don't want to go back. Anyway, you need to have time as a private citizen. One of the points of *The Edge* is that Washington is a terribly isolated place. The people there know each other, but too many of them have lost touch with the people back home. Politicians tend to be clubby people because they thoroughly distrust each other, and the clubbiest place of all is Congress. It is a subtle kind of clubbiness. It cuts across party lines, and a rebel on either side is considered a danger to both sides.

"Anyone who needs politics emotionally or financially should get out of the business. They are people who can't live without a narcotic, and the narcotic is power. Still, it's a tough bug, and it doesn't die easily."

If he's not interested in going back to politics, is John Lindsay going back to another novel? "Not now, not until I have something to say." What interests him most now, he says, is practicing law once again. Besides clients that take him to the Middle East, he also has some local cases to handle, including a lawsuit over a dog bite. "Know anything about torts? It's really a fascinating case. Every dog in New York City is allowed to bite someone once. One free bite, and after that the dog's in trouble. Except for German shepherds. They get no free bites, and the dog in my case is a German shepherd. So, it's all more complex than you might think. My partners, though, like to tease me about it. When they pass me in the hallway, they say, 'Woof, woof.' " (1976)

110.

ARNOLD and ANITA LOBEL

"I'm a professional illustrator," Arnold Lobel says, "and an amateur, lucky writer." However he categorizes himself, Lobel has turned out more than sixty children's books since he illustrated his first one seventeen years ago. "It all began with sixty-four pages of a salmon swimming upstream," he recalls. "It was the sort of thing no established illustrator would touch, but what did I know? I was just out of art school." More illustration assignments came in and in 1962, with *A Zoo for Mr. Muster*, he illustrated his own text for the first time. The book grew out of many visits he made to Brooklyn's Prospect Park zoo with his two young children. As he now remembers it, "They were particularly fond of the vultures and the ice cream."

He says he started writing purely for economic reasons. "The best way to make money in the children's-book business is to both write and illustrate. Then I found that I actually liked writing. When I'm old and infirm and my fingers start to shake, I'll only write. But for now, I write out the stories first, get them the way I want them and then illustrate them. I save the drawing for dessert." His most popular books are probably the Frog and Toad series, and he is one of the few writer-illustrators who have won both a Caldecott Honor Award (for the illustrations in *Frog and Toad Are Friends*) and a Newbery Honor Award (for the text of *Frog and Toad Together*).

His recent book, *Mouse Soup*, is in the Frog and Toad tradition in that it is a collection of short, connected stories for the 4- to 8-year-old group. Many children will be able to read the book themselves. It tells how a mouse, who is caught by a weasel and put into a soup pot, saves his neck by telling a series of outlandish stories. "I always wanted to do something with Scheherazade, but with kids I can't go on for 1001 nights and have a seduction. So, I turned to mice. They're small and vulnerable, and children seem to identify with

111.

them, mice and rabbits. For some reason I've never been able to do a rabbit story."

How the Rooster Saved the Day, the latest Lobel book, has a new byline: By Arnold Lobel—Pictures by Anita Lobel. "I've never had anyone illustrate my words before," Arnold says, "and seeing the result was a shock." Anita is Arnold's wife, a children's writer and illustrator with more than twenty books to her credit. Arnold continues: "I kept seeing things I wouldn't have done. I wanted to say, What have you done to my story? But I shut up and kept quiet, which is what all writers should do. If you want to draw, go to art school."

Anita agrees. "Most writers feel possessive about their words, but the one thing I asked Arnold to change, he changed without a fuss. And he was so handy. After all, he was right there across the room at his own drawing board." Arnold wrote the story in a week ("I took the money and ran," he says), and Anita spent six months on the illustrations. It is a "peasant tale"—to use Arnold's description—about a quick-witted rooster who outwits a dull-witted thief.

The Lobels work at facing tables in an airy top-floor studio in their Brooklyn brownstone. Since their children have gone off to school—Adrianne to Yale, Adam to Tufts—they share the house only with their aging pet turtle, who roams the place at will. Arnold's table is cluttered with sketches (chiefly of grasshoppers the day I visited) and layouts. Anita's is suspiciously tidy. She has lately been more involved in the theater than in books and not long ago played the title role in an Off Broadway production of Robinson Jeffers' *Medea*. "Can you imagine," she says, "a children's-book lady murdering little children?" She laughs, and Arnold laughs with her.   (1977)

JAMES McCONKEY

While James McConkey was writing *The Tree House Confessions*, his third novel, he spent a lot of time sitting in a tree house that he and one of his sons had built years ago on their upstate New York goat farm. "It's fairly roomy," he said recently, "and built over a deer trail. There's a cot and a table and a small porch, and like the tree house in the novel, the corners don't fit. It is a good place to go to think about things you would like to do or have to do. The novel deals with facing up to the death of a child, but the seed of it was really the time I spent thinking about how I was going to have to tell my mother that my father was dying."

In *The Tree House Confessions* a middle-aged newspaperman retreats to his son's old tree house after the death of his mother. There he reviews his life until he is able to accept not only the death of his mother but, more important, the earlier death of his son. The mother, in the novel, says memory gives one the power to hurt. McConkey agrees, adding, "But also the power to help. It is the saving grace, our basic impulse to pull things together."

McConkey teaches English literature at Cornell (Thomas Pynchon asked him to be his faculty adviser when Pynchon switched from engineering to English), and just about every seven years, he says, he produces a book. The first one was a study of the novels of E. M. Forster, who, along with Chekhov, remains his favorite author. Soon after the book was published he had a chance to meet Forster in his apartment at King's College, Cambridge. "It was terrible," McConkey recalls, "all very polite but terrible. We had tea and cake and Forster leaned forward and said he wanted to tell me about a grave mistake he had made as a young man. He said, 'I trusted people too much,' and I was shocked. I didn't want to believe that anyone, especially Forster, thought you could trust people too much. I was probably too young to believe it, so I said something about liking Beethoven's last quartets, and he said he preferred the earlier ones, and that was that."

Turning to his own books McConkey says, "I want to know that what I write helps, not hurts. I can't accept the notion that character—human identity—in fiction is banal and that the writer must find a way to get around it. Like the character in my novel, I believe carpentry is a very healthy thing. I think it is my impulse to repair." Which reminds me of something he said earlier, when we were talking about his 175-acre farm: "Farming isn't a matter of planting and plowing; it's a matter of fixing up broken machinery."

(1979)

GEORGE McGOVERN

In 1974, when every newspaper seemed to have new and more damning Watergate revelations, Pat Caddell, who had been George McGovern's official pollster in the 1972 presidential campaign, asked voters in California and Indiana whom they voted for in '72. Although Massachusetts was the only state McGovern carried in the actual election, he won Caddell's recount handily. "I wasn't all that surprised," McGovern said when he talked with me during a recent visit to New York. "Ever since Watergate became news, I've found it increasingly difficult to meet anyone who claims to have voted for Nixon."

The senator has just published his political autobiography. It is called *Grassroots*, and he believes it was the McGovern grassroots-style campaigning that got Jimmy Carter to the White House. "He studied our methods—and perhaps more important he studied our mistakes—and like us he went around the bosses and made his appeal directly to the grass-roots voters. I don't believe he ever would have made it if we hadn't blazed the trail."

Like McGovern, Carter used Caddell as his pollster. He used the same mail-order fund raiser and, again like Mc-Govern, announced his candidacy two years before the general election. McGovern points out that both of them promised to tell the truth, to cut the military budget, to decriminalize marijuana, to win fair treatment for draft resisters, even to clamp down on tax-deductible martini lunches. "I don't know how many people remember," Mc-Govern says, "but I too had a *Playboy* interview."

Grassroots follows McGovern's political career from the time he dropped out of graduate school and became executive secretary of the South Dakota Democratic party to his recent visits to such controversial world figures as Yasir Arafat and Fidel Castro. In trying to get a Democratic foothold in South Dakota in the early 1950s, he says his biggest problem was the few registered Democrats who were already there. "I had to overcome their sense of purity. You have no idea how pure it makes you feel being the only Democrat in a small South Dakota town."

But most of the book deals with McGovern's years in the Senate and the 1972 campaign. He says, "There is a mistaken impression that Vietnam dissent began on the campuses. Dissent originated in the Senate as early as 1964 with speeches by Wayne Morse and Ernest Gruening. The campuses didn't heat up until 1966, and by then the Senate was the place that actually focused antiwar feeling. I don't want to minimize what the kids did, but they came in later." Recently, though, he has noticed a growing sense of disillusionment with full-time politics among his congressional colleagues. "A line you hear often in the cloakroom these days is that politics isn't fun anymore. The process is too slow, they say, and the voters are too critical. A lot of congressmen are just not running for reelection, which means that there is going to be a very different Senate within the next few years."

About the '72 election, he says, "Vietnam tore the Democratic party to pieces. As long as the war was going on I doubt if any Democrat could have won. But at least Democrats debated the issues, just as we debated—and were torn apart by—the civil rights issue in the '60s. The war now has become the conversation no one wants to get into. The least we could do is to help reconstruct the country we destroyed. We did that with Germany and Japan, who were far less innocent than Vietnam. They, after all, attacked us; the Vietnamese wouldn't have harmed us if we had left them alone."

One of the few personal sections of *Grassroots* contains the senator's brief comments on his son and four daughters, and they seem to me to be tinged with regret. "Regret," he answers, "yes. I'm not a bad father, but I should have been better. I let the demands of political office take me away from them, and I think we were all harmed by that." His son, Steven, did not campaign for him in '72 because he dreaded the idea of being a president's son. "The day after the election," McGovern says, "he told his mother that if he knew I was going to lose he would have helped out. He just couldn't imagine his father not winning.

"One of the things I detect about our economy is that we may be producing our first generation that won't be more successful than its parents. I admired my father, but it never occurred to me that I wouldn't do better than he did. Just about everyone in my generation thought that way about their parents. Now, with the cost of everything being what it is, I wonder if we haven't come to the end of that spiral. And then what happens to the morale of the next generation?"

(1978)

LARRY McMURTRY

Larry McMurtry is the only novelist I know of who runs his own bookstore. It sells rare books, featuring 19th-century items, in the Georgetown section of Washington, D.C. McMurtry went to Washington six years ago because he heard it was a good place to finish a novel. The novel he was finishing was *Moving On*, but he liked the town so much he decided to stay put. He also takes a writer's interest in Washington. "There hasn't been a serious novel about Washington since Henry Adams wrote *Democracy* in the 1870s," he said recently. "I want to change that. The only trouble is that I seem to have a ten- or twelve-year time lag. I've finally finished writing about Texas. The book I'm working on now is set in California. I figure I won't get to Washington until some time after 1980."

His newly published novel, *Terms of Endearment,* a broad comedy with serious undertones about a Texas matron, is, McMurtry says, his literary farewell to his native state. His earlier Texas books include *Horseman, Pass By* (chapters of which were the basis for the film *Hud*), *The Last Picture Show* and *All My Friends Are Going to Be Strangers*.

"The bookstore," he says, "is a good balance to my writing. It's intellectually challenging but not emotionally demanding, and unlike writing you don't reach a peak and then dry up. The more you sell, the more you know." The book business, he says, grew out of his experience as a book accumulator. "Growing up in west Texas, where there just aren't many books around, made me want to own copies of all the books I read. After a while I found that I couldn't afford to buy new ones unless I sold some of the old ones. At a very early age I became something of a book dealer. Later, when I was a graduate student at Stanford, I worked as a scout for some stores in San Francisco. The Washington store really grew out of that." He no longer collects books.

117.

"There's nothing like owning a store to cool the collecting urge."

His urge to read contemporary fiction has cooled as well. "The only new novels I read," he says, "are the ones I have to review for *The Washington Post*. I'm much happier reading 19th-century nonfiction, especially travel books." He sees the form of *Terms of Endearment* as having its roots in the 19th-century novel. "For 350 pages it is a comedy. Then there's a jump of nine years, and the last fifty pages are tragic. I like funny books that turn sad. It's a trick Thackeray liked to use, and I needed that kind of ending to bring the novel to a proper close, not just this novel but all the Texas novels."

His next novel, set in Hollywood, will probably owe something to McMurtry's experience as a film writer. His best-known script is *The Last Picture Show*, which was filmed, fittingly enough, in his hometown, Archer City, Texas. "The most interesting thing about film writing is rewriting under pressure. Getting the original script done is really quite mechanical. But once the camera starts rolling and last-minute changes have to be made, then things get interesting. After a week of shooting *The Last Picture Show*, it became clear that the movie as written was going to run well over three hours, so it had to be rewritten, cut a third, on the spot."

What, I wondered, was it like going home to make a movie of what seems to be a very autobiographical novel? McMurtry didn't answer for a long time and then said, "Let's just say that it was hard to get back to." His family still lives in Archer City, and his father was offered a small part in the film. He turned it down because it involved swearing. "He said his reputation was getting bad enough in town without cussin' on the screen."

We returned to the subject of combining book selling with book writing. "Regularity is the secret," he said. "I write five pages every morning and then go down to the store. If I stick to that schedule I write quite easily and I can get through the day without feeling guilty. The strange thing is that in the book trade my reputation as a dealer is a good deal better than my reputation as a novelist." (1976)

JOHN McPHEE

"**W**hat characterizes my work is a considerable miscellaneity," says John McPhee. "Or miscellaneousness, take your pick. Reviewers, though, seem compelled to put me in some sort of category. I've read that I'm a sportswriter or an outdoors writer, even an agricultural writer. Actually, I write about what interests me at the moment."

In the dozen books McPhee has published over the past ten years, he has written about such varied subjects as the Loch Ness monster, a prep school headmaster, Bill Bradley, the New Jersey pine barrens, Scotch whisky, Arthur Ashe, firewood, the Sierra Club and oranges. "*Oranges,* for some reason, is the book no one has forgotten. I suspect it's because it seems so outrageous to write an entire book on oranges. The way that book evolved, though, is typical of the way I work. I went down South to spend a week in an orange grove and ended up staying a month, and what began as a short 'Talk of the Town' piece for *The New Yorker* ended up as a book. People sometimes complain that the things I write are too long to be magazine articles and too short to be books. I don't know about that. Writing is not a structured business. I write on a subject until it reaches its natural length, and then I stop."

McPhee and I were talking in his office in Princeton. It is on the second floor of a bank building, just across the street from the university and just across the hall from a place that offers Swedish massages. McPhee has spent most of his life in Princeton. The son of a local doctor, he went to high school and college there and after spending five years in New York City came back home. His office has a nice sense of academic clutter about it. The shelves are crammed with bound books and yellowing galleys. The walls are covered with pictures by McPhee's three daughters and maps of Alaska. He is currently at work on a book about the western Brooks mountain range, north of the Arctic Circle, and will be returning there for his third visit this summer. Each spring he teaches a course in nonfiction writing at the university. "I'm a so-called visiting professor, but I'm neither a visitor nor a professor."

McPhee arrives at his office every morning at 8:30. "I hang around until 6:00 without much happening, and then between 6:00 and 8:00, things tend to get written. I figure that I write about 60,000 published words a year for *The New Yorker*. I find writing exasperatingly difficult, and increasingly so every year."

I had gone to Princeton to talk with McPhee about his new book, *The Survival of the Bark Canoe*, an account of a cantankerous young French Canadian named Henri Vaillancourt, who lives in southern New Hampshire and builds birchbark canoes, and of a canoe trip McPhee took with him in Maine. Vaillancourt is probably the only man in the country who still makes bark canoes, and I was curious about his reaction to the book. "I haven't the slightest idea of what he thought about it," McPhee said. "Or even if he read it. I haven't heard a word from him or the other people on the trip, which is unusual. I usually hear something—cries of outrage, anything—from the people I write about. You don't write these things *for* the people involved. But you can't help wondering about their reaction."

An even better introduction to John McPhee's work is another book he had published last year, *Pieces of the Frame*, eleven *New Yorker* essays that range from Scotland to Atlantic City to the Great Smoky Mountains National Park. It is a book that everyone interested in clear, seemingly effortless prose should read.

I told McPhee that I could not imagine his being published in any magazine other than *The New Yorker*. "You betcha," he said. "It allows me to be able to develop the way I want. There's no other magazine in the world that would print some of the things they do—and I write. I find that I can't write something that might not be published. When I have an idea, I go to Shawn and ask him if he wants it for the magazine. If he says yes, I do it. If he says no, that's that. Good ideas come along faster than you can cope with them. So I really don't mind if I have to junk one and move on."

Since most of his *New Yorker* pieces are based on interviews, I asked him if he ever used a tape recorder. "Never," he said. "Too many books in my field almost smell of tape. When you record, there are just too many words and there is a temptation to use them all. Writing is a selective process and you have to select from the very beginning. You, for instance, have taken notes of about 10 percent of what I've said this morning. You've been weeding out what you don't want or need."

I asked him about the Swedish massage parlor across the hall. "It's legitimate. An old Scandinavian couple run it, but lately they've been attracting customers looking for something they don't offer. Sometimes people who don't get what they expected come over and bang on my door. 'What do you want,' I ask them, 'an American massage?' " (1976)

HISAKO MATSUBARA

When Hisako Matsubara's novel was published in Germany it was called *Brokatrausch* (brocade fever). On this side of the Atlantic it is called *Samurai*. And in Japan—where the author, the daughter of a Shinto high priest, lived until she came to Penn State for graduate work in the theater—the book has yet to be titled because it hasn't been translated into Japanese. Hisako Matsubara wrote it in German.

"I thought of it in German," she said during a recent visit to

121.

the United States. "There are things I can say in German that I could never say in Japanese. There is a logic to the language that must be followed." She lives in Cologne, now, with her son and her husband, a chemist she met while studying in the United States. She is the author of two collections of short stories (in German) and has written and directed several television documentaries on Japanese subjects.

"In Germany," she says, "I discovered Heine. I was impressed by his mixture of irony and poetry, his sarcasm and bitterness. From Germany I saw a mixture of misery and sacrifice in Japan that I never saw at home. From Heine, of all people, I learned that you must sacrifice to keep tradition."

But she doesn't like to talk about misery and sacrifice in terms of *Samurai*. "I think it is a love story." It is a story based on her grandfather, Nagayuki, who was sent to America as a young man to make his fortune, alone as a samurai should, with the assumption that he would soon return to his village and his bride rich and "dressed in brocade." He did not return for 60 years, and when he did he was penniless. Matsubara remembers him as "a wrinkled old man, delicate in his manners and speech but with dreadfully overworked hands." His only comment on America was "You cannot change the flow of the stream."

"I knew my great-grandfather," she recalls, "the man who sent Nagayuki to America, only from pictures in a photo album. In some he wore costumes from Noh plays, so I knew he must have studied them. I knew that he raised bonsai trees and that he lost the family fortune. I made up the rest. To learn more about Nagayuki in America I studied at the Hoover Institution at Stanford University and interviewed almost 200 Japanese-Americans. But I found that the story in my novel was not what he did here but what my grandmother did as she waited at home with their daughter. The story is hers, and his is heard as an echo. In Shinto philosophy there is no life after death. All you can leave is your memory with those who love you."

Hisako Matsubara was trained as a Shinto priestess, but she practices that calling only when she assists her father during her annual three-month visit to Japan. She grew up on the grounds of the Kenkun Shrine in Kyoto ("a hill surrounded by thousands of pines, acorns and cherry trees right in the city," she says) and has no memories of World War II. "To have lived in Kyoto is not to have known the war. It was spared the bombings because of its ancient buildings. I do remember the occupation, though. As a little girl I remember the Westerners' legs as being very long."

In her visits to Japan she becomes, she says, completely Japanese, but when she returns to Germany things change. "I dream in German when I'm in Germany. Even the Japanese characters in my dreams speak German.

"There has always been a special relationship between Germans and Japanese. Sometimes old Germans, especially men, come up to me and say, 'Next time, without Italy,' and they laugh." (1980)

WILLIAM MAXWELL

I t has been 19 years since William Maxwell's last novel, *The Château*, was published, and it has been four years since he retired as a fiction editor of *The New Yorker*. His new book, *So Long, See You Tomorrow*, is fiction, but it is based on fact, a murder and suicide long ago in Lincoln, Illinois, Maxwell's hometown. The narrator, an old man looking back, says, "This memoir—if that's the right name for it—is a roundabout futile way of making amends."

It is one of the most American novels of the season, American in the sound of its speech, in its small-town setting and in its sense of guilt. "I know evil exists," Maxwell said recently. "I have experienced it internally and externally, but I don't understand it enough to write about it." Instead he has written about good people who ache with loneliness and a feeling of sadness for having left undone what they ought to have done: a boy, for instance, who snubs his only friend after he learns that the boy's father had killed his mother's lover, a neighboring farmer and then himself.

The friendship between the narrator and the murderer's son is so understated that the boy could almost pass for an imaginary friend. "Alas," Maxwell says, "there was such a boy. If the incident in the high school corridor hadn't happened, if I hadn't passed him without speaking, I went a long way afield to get a story. The incident was true. The facts, as I say in the novel, came from old newspapers I tracked down in the Illinois State Historical Library. The newspaper itself, which is still publishing, had destroyed all its files and back issues. It was the paper I delivered as a boy. I remember that we had to wait outside in the snow for the presses to start running. They were always late. Even in the 1920s the presses were antiques. But reading old newspapers is maddening. They tell you so much you wish they would tell you more. They tell that the murdered man, who was milking a cow when he was shot, was wearing gloves. I wonder why. Maybe he had a skin condition. The papers never mention the name of the murderer's son."

Maxwell says he got over his uneasiness about describing farm life by writing out—and discarding—long accounts of how the farmers in his novel spent their time. "I wrote about them until I felt at ease with them. But that was only for myself. It is nothing for a reader to bother with." He worked as hard on perfecting the sound of Midwestern speech. "As I get older," he says, "the writers I prefer are the ones whose voices I can hear. Writing should seem as natural as speech, and for the best writers it is all one thing."

Maxwell was on *The New Yorker* staff for 40 years. He began in the art department as the person who told cartoonists whether their work had been accepted ("the feeling was that humor was nothing to be sneezed at") and later ("when they taught me to edit") he moved into the fiction department. "I loved working with other people's words," he recalls, "and I had the advantage of working only with very good writers. If I hadn't been an editor I probably would have written more, but not much more."

Over the years he has produced nine novels and short story collections and a book of family history. He is now at work on a collection of Sylvia Townsend Warner's letters. "I know it is an extravagant thing for a man of my age to be doing, but if I started to write another book now I'd just write the same story again in a different form. I have to wait for the well to fill up." (1980)

LEONARD MICHAELS

The 1950s, as Leonard Michaels sees them, ended on May 14, 1960. The day before, a small student demonstration at the House Un-American Activities Committee hearings being held in San Francisco exploded into what was labeled a riot. Mounted police moved in, and that night the newspapers were filled with photographs of officers dragging coeds down the elegant stairway of City Hall. The "riot" itself was in the disorganized spirit of the '50s. The '60s began the next day, when students from all over northern California converged on City Hall.

Michaels writes about what happened in his short story "In the Fifties": "The next morning I crossed the Bay Bridge to join my first protest demonstration. I felt frightened and embarrassed. . . . I expected to see thirty or forty people like me, carrying hysterical placards around the courthouse until the cops bludgeoned us into the pavement. About two thousand people were there. I marched beside a little kid who had a bag of marbles to throw under the hoofs of the horse cops. His mother kept saying, 'Not yet, not yet.' We marched all day. That was the end of the fifties."

"In the Fifties" is one of thirteen stories in Michaels' new collection, *I Would Have Saved Them if I Could*, one of the best collections of this, or any other, year. It deals with love and death and basketball, city life and Lord Byron, but mostly it is about how life in America was somehow different after that May Saturday in San Francisco.

Michaels, who teaches at the University of California at Berkeley, was in New York recently and we talked about the 1950s. "We were silent," he recalls, "but we were interesting to one another. We hadn't been politicized, and we had an intimacy that's been lost. Love has now become an aspect of ideology. One's sexuality is now even a political statement." Intimacy is probably the key word in understanding Michaels' view of the '50s. He sees what has happened to his old Manhattan high school as almost symbolic of that lost intimacy. "The place," he says, "has become audience-conscious. In the old days you went there because you were an artist. You could paint or play a musical instrument better than kids who went to other schools. I went there because everyone, my parents and teachers, thought I was a good painter. I thought I was something special, but at the High School of Music and Art I discovered there were kids more talented than I, that there was real talent in this world, real standards. But this was all a personal thing. Now, it seems, the kids are trained to win response from the crowd. They're being made into servants of applause."

Our conversation turned to the short-story form. The new book is Michaels' second collection of stories, and he teaches the history of the short story at Berkeley ("from the Book of Genesis to Flannery O'Connor"). He believes that a short story, more than any other literary form, is dependent on its ending. "The ending must be implicit in the beginning." He also decries the popular notion that these are bad days for short-story writers. "The opportunity for publication is better than ever before. There must be 1000 little magazines in this country, a fantastic opportunity for writers. Of course, most of them won't pay you anything." Then he adds, as most short-story writers seem to add, that he's at work on a novel.

I asked him what it was like being back home in New York after living for years in California. "I'll give you two images that seem to sum up the place. The other night we were driving down Seventh Avenue and suddenly standing in front of us was this huge, blond Viking-looking guy. We had to swerve to miss him and he just stood there, as though he were waiting to be hit. We looked back and he was still standing in the street, waiting for the next car, or maybe next after that, to run him down. The other image was a huge pothole in the middle of the street, with a white line painted through it. That's the ultimate cynicism, a white line painted through a pothole."

Our conversation turned naturally from the city to basketball, a game that appears in a number of Michaels' stories. "Basketball *is* the city. My whole adolescence was tied up with it. Everything good about the city is synthesized in a great basketball player like Walt Frazier: grace, power, immense confidence. I sometimes think about throwing a party and inviting Walt Frazier. I wonder if he'd come."

(1975)

BRIAN MOORE

Brian Moore is the author of nine novels, among them *The Lonely Passion of Judith Hearne*, *The Luck of Ginger Coffey* and most recently *The Great Victorian Collection*. The question is, how do you pronounce his first name? No matter how you do it, there is always someone to correct you. Does it rhyme with "freein'," as it is pronounced in Northern Ireland, where Moore spent his first twenty-seven years? Or with "fryin'," as it is pronounced in Canada and the United States, where Moore has spent his past twenty-seven years?

Moore was in New York not so long ago, and I put the question to him. The answer was not a simple one. He and his family and many of his friends pronounce it in the Irish manner, but he would prefer people to use the North American pronunciation. "I sometimes think when people hear 'Breean Moore, the writer' they don't associate the name with 'Brian Moore, the writer.' "

He suspects this confusion reflects a greater confusion about him and his work. "My career has suffered," he says, "because I've never been tagged and put in a category. I'm not thought of as Irish or Canadian or American. I live in California, but I'm a Canadian citizen. I have been one for years, but many Canadians still call me a New Canadian. Moore is an Irish Protestant name, but I was born a Catholic even though I don't practice Catholicism anymore. A lot of Irish think I'm Protestant, and Alfred Hitchcock supposedly hired me as a screenwriter because he thought my novel *Feast of Lupercal* was anti-Catholic. Then when *Catholics* came out in 1973, some critics suddenly decided I was a Catholic writer. None of this helps your readers. They like to identify you with a race or a country."

The Great Victorian Collection, Moore's newest novel, deals with a Canadian with an Irish name—a specialist in Victorian history at McGill University in Montreal—who while touring in California spends a night at a motel in Carmel, dreams and wakes to find that the wealth of Victoriana he dreamed about has materialized in the motel's parking lot. It is surely the greatest Victorian collection in America, perhaps the world, but how can he explain what happened? Who will believe him?

The novel is one of those rare fantasies that work. It is believable, and it entertains and finally becomes downright frightening. One is tempted to call the book an allegory, but Moore warns against using the word. "Allegory," he says, "is something no one reads." Then he adds a But. "But what would happen if a miracle occurred today? We seem to have lost our capacity for wonder, and I suspect we would diminish it because we couldn't understand it. What if our dreams come true? Failure actually makes people more intensely themselves, while success dehumanizes. The successful person can never really go home again. Look at the Canadians who come to the States and find success. They can't go back to Canada."

He also suggests a literary interpretation of the novel: "If you create, if you write, you are the prisoner of the work people know you by. *The Lonely Passion of Judith Hearne* was a book that took me years to get over. It was never a best seller, but I'd receive letters and phone calls about it from lonely people." In recent years those letters have become angry because Moore has refused to write more lonely passions. "I'd rather gamble on something different."

It was Alfred Hitchcock who brought Moore to Southern California after he had lived for eight years in New York. Together, Moore and Hitchcock wrote the screenplay for *Torn Curtain*. "It was awful, like washing floors," Moore recalls. He wrote another, unproduced script but swears he will never do another. (He predicts that TV will become the avant-garde medium as the movies become more ossified.) He did, though, discover a house near Malibu—"more deserted than Ireland"—and spends eight months a year there, writing. "If you are writing novels you need a cave of dullness, and L.A. is one of the most amorphous cities in the world, an excellent place for novelists."

Recently he took a trip up the coast to see Carmel, the setting for *The Great Victorian Collection*, and he visited the local library. They had a number of his books, which had obviously been read. "But they were utterly clean, unbelievably clean. The cleanest people on earth must live in that town."   (1975)

INDIANA NELSON

"Tucson," said Indiana Nelson the other day, "is one of those places that always looks spelled wrong." Born and raised on a cattle ranch, she was packed off to school in Massachusetts and California ("I had the worst education of any white woman I know") but returned to Tucson to make something of a name for herself as a painter of impressionistic landscapes. In those days she called herself Dianne. Indiana came later, after she spent four years sketching trucks at a diesel repair shop on the outskirts of Tucson. It's a nickname that came not from the state ("I've never been across the Indiana state line"), but from a Mexican maid who had trouble remembering "Dianne." "Even my mother now calls me Indiana," she said during a recent visit to her New York art gallery, "so it must be the right name for me."

The time she spent sketching at the repair shop resulted in no impressionistic paintings but in a realistic novel, *Truckstop*, that deals touchingly and with good humor with the lives of women who live at the truckstop. "The idea for a novel really came from the woman I call Mabel in the book. She was the grande dame of the place, and she kept inviting me over to her trailer to talk. She thought she was a sexpot, but really she looked like an over-the-hill Mae West. She was a wonderful woman, but oh did she hate trucks. 'Why do you draw those ugly old things?' she'd ask me. 'Why don't you draw a picture of me so people will remember what I look like after I'm dead?' But I was afraid if I drew her the way she really looked she would just die. So I kept on drawing the trucks. I'd do them at night because it was cooler then and they didn't want me around during the day. As I sketched I sometimes wrote down what the truckers and repairmen were saying. I began to think of what I was doing as truck ballads."

A good deal of that conversation made it into her novel intact, as did a number of the sketches themselves, but it was Mabel who became the heart of the book, "She kept telling me stories, and she'd have me drive her to the Alcoholics Anonymous meetings in Tucson, which is where you heard all the best talk in town. She died without me ever doing a picture of her, so I began writing down her stories and the men's talk and the AA gossip, and after a while, to my surprise, I had what my friends said was a novel."

(1980)

JACQUES PEPIN

Jacques Pépin was 13 when his parents, proprietors of a small restaurant in Lyons, apprenticed him to the head chef of the Grand Hôtel de l'Europe in Bourg-en-Bresse. In the twenty-six years since that apprenticeship began, Pépin has worked at the Meurice and the Plaza-Athénée in Paris and at Le Pavillon in New York. He also cooked in the French Navy, acted as director of research and develop-

131.

ment for Howard Johnson and served as Charles de Gaulle's *chef de cuisine* at the Elysée Palace. He is, Craig Claiborne says, "one of the most remarkable cooking talents of our time."

He has very strong views on professionalism in cooking. "It is one thing to love to cook," he said the other day, "but it's another to keep the love affair going seven days a week. Cooking is a craft—it takes craftsmanship and training."

We were talking in the kitchen of the rebuilt Catskill farmhouse where Pépin now lives with his wife and young daughter. The house is on a steep hill above the Schoharie Creek, and in the distance looms Hunter Mountain with its extensive network of ski trails. Pépin, for the sheer fun of it, has been a part-time ski instructor at Hunter for the past nine years. "Look," he said, gesturing toward the creek and another farm beyond. "It's like Grandma Moses, but it's even better when there's snow."

Pépin's new book, *A French Chef Cooks at Home*, is a collection of more than 150 recipes that he has cooked at home for friends. "It's a great way to try out something new," he says. The recipes, which include both simple and advanced dishes, range from basic sauces to lobster bisque to stuffed bass with herbs to saddle of lamb provençal to fresh noodles to strawberries with raspberry sauce.

Pépin doesn't believe in that old saying about too many cooks. While we talked, he and his wife, Gloria, were preparing for an evening dinner party built around a crusted lamb stuffed with spinach. It was the first time he had prepared the dish and he was making notes as he worked. I asked Gloria if most of their meals were joint ventures. "Well," she said, "I have my little jobs, Jacques has his big jobs, and our little girl makes the vinaigrette."

"She makes excellent vinaigrette," Pépin added, looking up from his notebook.

"Where are the potato peels?" Gloria asked.

"I threw them out." A large plastic garbage can on wheels stands at the center of the Pépins' bright, tiled kitchen.

"How do you expect to have a mulch pile if you always throw out the potato skins?"

Pépin turned the conversation to La Nouvelle Cuisine, the supposedly revolutionary method of French cooking that eschews cream, eggs and flour in favor of simplicity and fewer calories. "It is a mixture of nonsense, publicity and nothing much that's new. They claim to be attacking Escoffier. Big deal. He died forty years ago. But it was Escoffier whose motto was *faîtes simple* (keep it simple), and I can show you menus of his that are just like the ones the Nouvelle people claim to have invented. As for nonsense, take their theory that you can make sauces by reduction, by simply boiling and not adding flour. It doesn't work. You can boil all you want and you won't get a sauce. You'll get a flavoring."

He is against a narrow reading of Escoffier, however. "If he said to do something just because in his day there was no refrigeration, it is pointless to continue doing that today. If something tastes good, it's good."

Literal-mindedness, he feels, has harmed many cookbooks. "I once read in the page proofs of a book I had written that one should pat dry the inside of a chicken after you washed it. Ridiculous. I've never patted dry the inside of a chicken in my life. It's a waste of time. I challenged the editor, and she said it was something she added. She said that people were used to reading that in recipes and that if they didn't see it they'd feel uncomfortable."

Pépin shrugged and continued, "But it's a great pain in the neck to follow a recipe. Ideally you don't cook by a book but by your taste buds. Still, cooking is a vanishing art. Literally. You cook, they eat, and then there's nothing. Maybe that's why we want to write cookbooks, so there will be something left after all." (1976)

133.

S. J. PERELMAN

"If people expect me to be funny, they are in for a rude shock. I figure my job ends when I leave the typewriter and get out of the swivel chair. People make a mistake when they confuse a writer with a performer."

The speaker is S. J. Perelman, author of a new book called *Vinegar Puss*. He is sitting in the living room of his sparely furnished apartment overlooking Gramercy Park in Manhattan. On the walls are hung a few Saul Steinberg drawings and several maritime maps of Indonesia. Centered on one of the maps is the island of Ceram, a port in the Banda Sea that Perelman visited twenty years ago and still dreams of as the site of a retirement home. "The only guidebook to the place was published in 1856 by a friend of Darwin's," Perelman says, "and it is still up to date."

The room has an air of transience about it, a sense that fully packed suitcases are stacked in the closets. In fact, Perelman is about to leave on a nine-month around-the-world tour which should be considerably more leisurely than his last circumnavigation of the globe. That eighty-day dash is chronicled ("Around the Bend in Eighty Days") in *Vinegar Puss*, a distinctly tart collection of essays that deal, chiefly, with Perelman's recent Babylonian captivity in Britain.

In 1970 he announced that the United States—and New York in particular—was getting too brutal for him and that he was off to England and civilized living. A few years later he was back in town, muttering that it was impossible to find a good corned beef on rye in all of Albion.

Perelman claims that his exile was never intended to be permanent. "I went to investigate the clichés about the gentility of the English. I had done English bits before. But I found when I actually lived there that the place didn't seem so bizarre and eccentric as it did from over here."

As for New York: "It was bad when I left it and it hasn't gotten any better."

The eighty-day trip was an attempt to duplicate the events of Phileas Fogg's famous race with time. In 1956 Perelman had won an Academy Award for his script for Mike Todd's version of *Around the World in Eighty Days,* so it was a subject that interested him. "Also," he says, "like Fogg I am a member of the Reform Club in London."

For his own variation on the Jules Verne story, however, Perelman had decided to hire a beautiful young Amazon (from Pass Christian, Mississippi) for the Passepartout role. This wasn't his first experience with female luggage carriers. Years before, while in Africa writing some *New Yorker* pieces, he had seen a sign advertising for fifteen women to form the first all-girl safari. He had promptly signed up and marched across Uganda with them.

He is not optimistic about the new crop of comic writers: "The prospect is bleak. It's a form that seems doomed, the Ring Lardner–Benchley tradition. Woody Allen is sometimes good. Mel Brooks is good when he is doing the 2000-year-old man. Russell Baker is the most active, but I think you can say that the last couple of generations haven't been much interested in verbal gaiety."

As for Perelman's famous use of unusual words, he says: "I don't go out of my way to search for exotic words, but I think writers should use words that have exact meanings. I do like unfamiliar words and I use a thesaurus. It might even startle a reader into looking up what the words really mean."

A final question: Is S. J. Perelman himself a vinegar puss? He just looks out the window, off toward the Players Club across Gramercy Park, and smiles.   (1975)

HAROLD PINTER

When Harold Pinter, the British playwright, agreed to do a screenplay of Proust's *Remembrance of Things Past*, he had read only one of the novel's seven volumes and that was years before. "It takes a hell of a lot of time," he said the other day in a telephone call from his home in London. "I had taken the first volume, *Du Côté de Chez Swann*, from the library, and when I brought it back they hadn't the second, so I stopped right there. Like most people who have gone that far, I kept saying to myself, 'I must read the whole damn thing sometime.' When Joe Losey asked me to do the screenplay I got my chance to put my feet up and read it steadily for three months. Even at the beginning I felt pretty Proustian, so it was like getting back to an old friend. Then came nine months of work of my own on it."

Those twelve months, he says, made up the "best writing year of my life."

All this began in 1972. The film was never made, but the finished text has finally been published under the title *The Proust Screenplay*. The title page credits Pinter as having written it "with the collaboration" of Joseph Losey (the film director with whom Pinter worked on *The Servant, Accident* and *The Go-Between*) and Barbara Bray (a BBC editor who is an authority on Proust).

"I felt Proust to be purely cinematic," Pinter continued. "The crucial images—the involuntary recall of memory— are extremely visual. He actually refers to the cinema in the last volume of the novel and says it can't work as an art form because everything is too much on the surface. I think he is wrong. I wish he were alive so I could discuss the screenplay with him. I think you *càn* show the underlying play of emotion and memory on film."

Twelve years ago, in an interview in *The Paris Review*, Pinter said that he felt his job as a writer was to "follow the clues." As an interpreter of Proust he finds the job more complex. "It was an excavation," he says. "You have to un-earth the themes and the motifs within the themes. It was archaeological, a search for hidden treasures and their relation-ships." In such plays as *The Birthday Party*, *The Caretaker* and *The Homecoming*, Pinter has become known for intricate word play, but with Proust he has moved away from the play of language to the play of images and sound: a bell on a garden gate, an uneven paving stone, the sight of the sea from a hotel room, three church steeples seen from a train, a girl's laughter in a hedgerow, a yellow wall in a Vermeer painting. Finally, it was Pinter's task to distill 3000 pages of Proust to a 177-page filmscript.

But Pinter stresses the fact that the screenplay was written to be filmed. "I regard the script as a piece of art, but it has a very practical purpose. I acted it out with my son—he was about 14 at the time—and we played the whole film using a stopwatch. We acted all the parts, even the church steeples, and I tell you it sounded pretty good."

Running time? "Three and a half hours, almost on the nose." (1978)

DAVID PLANTE

David Plante speaks with a soft, precise British accent that he didn't have when he left his home in one of the French Canadian neighborhoods of Providence, Rhode Island, in the early 1960s. It's something he picked up while living in London. "Thirteen years leave a marking," he said during a recent visit to the United States, "and I guess I'm marked." He used that time writing six novels, the first five of which are as foreign to Providence as his new accent. His sixth, *The Family*, has just been published, and it is triumphant proof that, if you really want to, you can go home again.

"In my early novels," he says, "beginning with *The Ghost of Henry James*, I wanted to write books that didn't refer to anything outside themselves. I succeeded so well that my fifth novel, which hasn't been published over here, isn't set anywhere at all. I love silence and mystery in fiction, and with *The Family* I wanted to write a book with a specific setting, a straight novel that still kept those silences."

The silences in his novel are those that fall amid the arguments and monologues of a large French Canadian family in Providence. There are five sons, a father who—unlike all his friends—is antiunion and a Republican, and a mother who has watched most of her dreams come to nothing. "I can't say it's my family. It's not, but I'm not giving them copies of the book until the day before I go back to London."

He says he lives there not out of any sense of expatriation but because it is a place where he cannot take anything for granted. "When you begin doing that you're in trouble. Since I'm not English I can't take for granted that I understand anything that's happening around me, and since I'm in the States only once a year I can't take things for granted there either. Before I settled in London I studied at the University of Louvain, in Belgium, and I seem to have lost my ability to speak French Canadian. Maybe I've even lost my sense of being French Canadian.

"French Canadian culture in the States may be one of the most closed minorities in the country. It is probably the largest minority in New England, but they have no special holidays or restaurants or music or anything. There is no sense of identity with France or Canada, nothing special but their language and the church, which is an especially dull form of Jansenism. But this makes it very easy for us to identify with other cultures. We have no limiting identity, so we can live anywhere."   (1978)

138.

SAM POSEY

It's probably just as well that young Sam Posey didn't name his sled Rosebud. What kid named Posey could get away with a sled named Rosebud? His was named The Mudge Pond Express, after a pond near his grandmother's estate in northwestern Connecticut. The Express had wheels mounted on it, and Posey used to race it over a tricky course he constructed in his basement. When he was 19 he bought his first racing car, something called a Jocko, and began racing on a local track. Later came a VW-powered Formcar, a Porsche 904 and others, and by the time he was 25 he was making it on his own—without his family's money— in professional racing. Today, at 32, he's near the top as a driver, although he admits that he rarely wins the big races. His critics claim he is too rich to care about winning. On a recent visit to New York City he said, "Sometimes I think I value speed itself over winning races."

Posey has just published a frank and entertaining history of his racing career called, logically enough, *The Mudge Pond Express*. "Most auto racing books," he says, "are ghosted for drivers who have made it big and tell how they did it. The reader knows all the time that they will end with some flashy win at Indy. I wanted to write my own book, one that wasn't about making it big but about the process of racing itself. I wanted to re-create what goes on in my mind while I race. It's one sport in which you aren't coached. If you make a mistake you make it on a $100,000 machine, and you can get killed for making it. Also, I'm one of the great losers in racing. I've lost all the big ones, but I've also won enough to know what losing means. If you've only been a loser you can never understand that."

He has raced at Le Mans, Watkins Glen, Sebring, Lime Rock, Indianapolis. He has raced independently and on the Chrysler team. Currently on the BMW team, he competes chiefly in Europe (about a hundred racing hours a year) and lives in Southern California. He's also a professional painter with a degree from the Rhode Island School of Design.

"Racing is strictly art for art's sake. There are few things more useless than a racing car. But from the very beginning I knew that racing was my one chance to be all I could be. I knew that if I didn't race nothing else would work out for me. I was tremendously lucky in that I had the money and the physical skill to do it. Imagine having all that desire and none of the ability."

Posey has recently been competing in European road races and I asked him how they compared with Indianapolis, which is a series of identical turns and straightaways. "In road racing the challenge is the blind turns, aiming at an apex you can't see. But Indy, in its way, is even more challenging. You seem to be driving the same race over and over again, but you aren't. You have to be especially good because you're driving against men who are getting just as familiar with the track as you are; there's a constantly changing pattern of oil spills; and your car is constantly changing weight. When it's full of gas it weighs 400 pounds more than when it's empty. Each time around the track is different, and it's terribly hard to see anything.

"Off the race track I'm really a chicken. I hate flying and have never had any interest in sky diving or hang gliding or any of those things people kill themselves doing. But I've never thought of speed as frightening. When you race you feel that you live on a different level from other people. Drivers are notorious for their extreme egotism. At Indy, for instance, it is the pit stops that are disorienting. You come to realize that your normal speed is 180 mph, that going any slower is unnatural."

Posey says he thinks next year will be his last as a racer. "I'd hate to think that my life as a driver just dragged on. I've now done about all I'm going to do, so it wouldn't be so dumb to get out. Still, it's kind of scary giving up what you're good at. A race is so much less complicated than life. Not more childish but more simple and direct. I can look at the statistics and know exactly where I stand as a driver. As a painter I can't do that. I think that's why people like to watch races: it's so much less complicated than their own lives. Lives don't boil down to numbers and a grade."

After our interview Posey was going off to see Frank Stella, the painter, who was designing the decorations for Posey's next car for BMW. Alexander Calder did last year's. Then he was going up to Mudge Pond to see his family and then back to the racing circuit. He didn't seem at all like a young man on the brink of retirement.   (1976)

REYNOLDS PRICE

Reynolds Price has published three novels, and if you add up their total number of pages (195 plus 275 plus 143) you'll get 613. Next month he will be publishing a new novel, *The Surface of Earth*, and with its 512 pages, he is going to just about double his output as a novelist in one fell swoop.

The Surface of Earth follows the sometimes complex comings and goings of a divided Southern family, a family that has both white and black branches. Price said recently that it is a book he planned to write as far back as 1962, just after his first novel, *A Long and Happy Life*, was published. "I tried to make it my second novel, about the summer of 1934 and a father and son, but every time I started it I realized I had to go back farther in time to explain how things got to be as they were." The finished book begins in 1903.

Price also found that his method of writing changed for this novel. For his earlier books he had made detailed notes and outlines. *A Long and Happy Life*, he says, was so carefully planned that when he finally came to write it, "it was just like filling in a coloring book."

He found the writing of *The Surface of Earth* more fun. "My method was to write at one page until I liked it and then move on to the next. I had no idea how it would end until I got there, although after I'd finished a hundred pages I knew I'd have to keep a card index to keep the characters straight." The book took four years to write. "Now that I'm in my 40s I've come to realize that my unconscious really does the writing and I just sit down every day and take the dictation."

Price was born in North Carolina and, except for an interlude at Oxford as a Rhodes scholar, has spent much of his life in and around Duke University. He teaches there today and lives in a small house in the woods near the campus. Teaching, he feels, is good discipline for a writer. "Look at the old generation of writers, the generation of Hemingway, Fitzgerald and Wolfe. They had little to do but write, and their free time was so badly spent, getting drunk and changing wives." He despairs, though, over the little reading—outside of assignments and certain fad books—being done by college students. "Private colleges," he says, "are becoming so expensive that the students are returning to the old country club attitudes of the 1920s. You would sometimes think the '60s never happened."

He continues, "I spent my childhood being raised by two Negroes who were born slaves, and they told me stories about the old days. They seemed to feel that they were somehow responsible for the whites. I suspect that's how the blacks survived slavery, by believing they were our moral tutors, our consciences. Their influence can be found in all my books."

Price's memory of stories of the old days told to him as a child did much to mold the shape and content of *The Surface of Earth*. The book contains a number of tragic childbirth scenes. "I was fascinated," he recalls, "by countless stories of dreadful births. People have forgotten that until the end of World War II childbirth was a very dangerous thing, and I think that had a great influence on men's ideas of women: that by being born—and by being fathers—they endangered women. It's a point feminists should become interested in."

Price believes that Southerners are especially adept—and practiced—storytellers. "My family were nonstop storytellers. As a child I didn't actually see much of what went on in the world, but I heard a great deal. Life, after all, is made up pretty much of a series of people telling what they think has happened. Just about everything happens offstage, and most of what we know is what people have told us about what they think has happened. What a person thinks to be the story of his life, that's what interests me most, what I want to write about."   (1975)

GREGORY RABASSA

The typical translator, Gregory Rabassa says, is all too often thought of—when he's thought of at all—as someone like Bob Cratchit, a faceless nonentity monotonously toiling away in a dark corner. But that stereotype is changing, and Rabassa's own translations of Spanish- and Portuguese-language authors (*The New York Times* recently called him "one of the best translators who ever drew breath") have played a key role in encouraging the change.

Since 1965, Rabassa has translated fifteen books by such authors as Julio Cortázar, Miguel Angel Asturias and Mario Vargas Llosa. He won a National Book Award in 1967 for his version of Cortázar's *Hopscotch*, but he is probably best known for the English-language editions of Gabriel García Márquez' *One Hundred Years of Solitude* and, more recently, *The Autumn of the Patriarch.*

"The most difficult thing about teaching translation," Rabassa said the other day at the Graduate Center of the City University of New York, "is the teaching of English. After all, when you put a page of Balzac into English you're much more involved with English than you are with French. A translator must first of all be able to write in his own language."

Rabassa says he does the first drafts of his translations with a dictionary at hand. "I work rapidly for accuracy and come up with something that reads almost like Pidgin English. I go back, after that, without the original text in front of me and polish. Then, it's back to the original. First I try to make it close, and then I try to make it nice. The third draft is the so-called finished copy, but then I go on and make fourth, fifth and sixth drafts."

He works differently with different authors. "Cortázar," he says, "is almost a collaborator in the translation. He likes to keep his hand in, and if he finds he cannot explain what he means he draws pictures with arrows and says, 'Make it like this.' Sometimes his manuscripts are covered with sketches. He also enjoys last-minute changes. In *Hopscotch* I mistakenly wrote 'fried eggs' as 'fired eggs.' He loved it, so we left it in. With García Márquez things are different. He doesn't have a strong understanding of English. He just says to me, 'Do what you want.' In *The Autumn of the Patriarch* there are eight words for which I could find no translation, and he couldn't help me on it. The novel finally had to go to press, so I made something up. I'll be hearing from at least one Spanish teacher on that, I'm sure. But then, foreign-language teachers are no judges of translations."

Rabassa was raised in western New Hampshire. His mother, he says, was "an eighth-generation New York WASP" and his father a Cuban who lost his family's sugar fortune in the crash of 1929 and turned their old summer home near Hanover into an inn. "All the Dartmouth Spanish professors would come over for Cuban meals." He graduated from

Dartmouth and then went on to Columbia, where he received his Ph.D. in Portuguese.

Rabassa would like to see more books translated into English before they are accepted for publication. "As things now stand, editors must decide whether or not to publish books they usually can't read. This is the weakest link in the publication of foreign books. Editors who would normally form their own opinions have to rely on the opinions of others, who all too often turn out to be local language teachers. Pre-translation, I know, would be expensive, but think of the possibilities for discovering new, and perhaps unlikely, authors."

If there is one thing about translating that depresses Rabassa, it is that translations don't wear well. "I'm talking about classics," he says, "but translations date faster than their originals. Almost from the beginning there have been excellent translations of *Don Quixote*. I think a general rule of translation is that good books get good translations, and bad books get bad ones. But in a hundred years or so a translation dies and a new one is needed, which, to look on the bright side, means that there will always be work for translators."

(1977)

MORDECAI RICHLER

The apprenticeship of Duddy Kravitz began on St. Urbain Street in the ghetto of Montreal in the 1940s. It's pretty safe to say the same is true of Duddy's creator, Mordecai Richler. Like Duddy, he grew up on St.

Urbain Street, went to the local high school, marched with the school air cadet corps ("They go the limit with guys in uniform, see"), shot snooker at the Laurentian Pool Hall, played ball on Fletcher's Field and hung out at Tansky's lunch counter, which had the most active telephone booth on the block.

While Duddy went his way as a streetwise hustler, Richler went off to college and then for a prolonged stay in England, where he began to write novels. His books include *Son of a Small Hero*, *The Apprenticeship of Duddy Kravitz*, *Cocksure* and *St. Urbain's Horseman*, most of which bear traces of the old neighborhood. Richler returned to Montreal in 1968 and almost immediately found himself in the midst of a curious public debate as to how authentically Canadian he really was. He also found that he had become one of the best-known Canadian writers of his generation.

I recently walked down St. Urbain with Richler and we talked about the area and *The Street*, his new book (new in the United States—it was published in Canada six years ago). A careful mixture of autobiographical essays and short stories, *The Street* is a unique, amusing and often moving portrait of a small corner of Montreal and its citizens.

St. Urbain is a wide street with high curbs and narrow sidewalks. The facades of its three- and four-story brick and stone houses are busy with a Victorian clutter of dormers, balconies, bay windows and ornamental ironwork. The total effect is almost American Southern. "When I first saw New Orleans," Richler says, "I was reminded of St. Urbain." Most of the houses have steep metal stairs leading from the street to the second floor. "They're fine for sitting on in summer," he adds, "but hell to keep shoveled in winter." Looming over all is Mount Royal with its huge cross made of steel girders.

The neighborhood is no longer Jewish. The former YMHA is now a branch of the city university; the Young Israel Synagogue is gone; if the most popular immigrant bank still has Hebrew signs in the window, the languages you hear inside are Greek and Portuguese. "The Jews," Richler says, "have moved to more modern ghettos, but the funny thing is that the grandchildren of the Jews who first settled on St. Urbain are now returning. They're students and they like the old buildings and the cheap rent."

When *The Apprenticeship of Duddy Kravitz* was being filmed on St. Urbain, Richler came to realize how little the neighborhood had changed. Tansky's had closed, but there was a diner around the corner that served just as well. "All we had to do was cover the Greek signs with Hebrew ones and shoot around the modern streetlights. The biggest problem was aluminum storm windows. We had to cover them up or take them out. Other than that, the high school, the streets and everything else looked just as they did in the '40s." *The Apprenticeship* turned out to be the most successful Canadian picture ever made. Richler was nominated for an Academy Award for his filmscript.

I asked him about the old debate over his Canadianness. "That's pretty much a thing of the past," he said. "There are still some nationalists who claim I write for foreigners, for export, rather than for Canadians, which is silly. Every now and then I'm criticized by people who think I'm exploiting my past, but they are people who confuse exploitation with the fact that one learns from one's experiences."

We stopped for lunch at the Montreal Hebrew Delicatessen. "This is a place that hasn't changed at all. Have the smoked meat sandwich. It's like pastrami, you'll like it." Some high school girls at the next table recognized Richler and went through an elaborate pantomime of nudging each other and silently mouthing his name: Mor-de-cai Richler. I said to him that we'd been talking about Greeks and Jews and WASPs and the French ("Montreal really isn't any more French than it used to be, it's just that the French are no longer afraid to speak out"), but I wondered who it was that really ran the city. Richler thought for a minute and then said, "I think it's probably the Scots, but you never see them."

(1975)

MAY SARTON

May Sarton is a loner. She has made a career out of it. Now in her middle 60s, she has published nearly thirty volumes of poetry, fiction and children's stories. Because she has avoided or escaped being identified with any particular school or faction in the poetry world, she lacks a claque, but she has made her presence known: those essays, poems and journals on the value of solitude; those photographs of her, a gray-haired woman striding through the tall grass alone; those rumors from homosexual and feminist circles that one of her novels, *Mrs. Stevens Hears the Mermaids Singing*, said it all long before it was fashionable to say it at all.

Now, after decades of celebrating the solitary life, she has published a celebration of friendship, *A World of Light*, a memoir of her parents, of girlhood friends in Europe, of New England neighbors and of some famous writers (Virginia Woolf, Elizabeth Bowen, Louise Bogan). She came down from her home in Maine the other day to talk about her new book and the value of friendship.

"Solitary people," she said, "have good friends because they have more to give in friendship. They have time for friendship. You don't have to make room for strangers; the room is there. Perhaps because I was an only child I have romanticized family life, but I believe it is very hard to be a woman artist and a wife and mother. The artist is a monster, perhaps a *monstre sacré*, but I believe it is easier for a man to be a monster. It is more socially acceptable. If you want to be a creative woman and a wife, you are just creating conflict."

With the publication three years ago of her collected poems and the reissue of some of her early novels (particularly *The Small Room* and *Mrs. Stevens Hears the Mermaids Singing*), Miss Sarton has been discovered by a younger audience. It is a new experience for her and she says she's thoroughly enjoying it. "It used to be that it was the older writers who praised my work and patted me on the head like parents. Now the young people are discovering me and writing me letters. I suspect they think that because I live alone I get lonely and would be cheered up by hearing from them. And I do like hearing from them. Even little children write. There are four children, brothers and sisters, who have been writing to me since they were 6. We'd never met, so after my most recent children's book, *A Walk Through the Woods*, came out I wrote to them and asked them to come to Maine and walk with me along the beach at York. They came and we had a fine picnic."

An older writer whose approval Miss Sarton sought was Virginia Woolf. "She was the only person whose opinion of my work really mattered. She was a sensitive woman but not at all warm. That was something of a shock. I had thought all sensitive people were warm. I still have dreams about her. In one dream she didn't commit suicide at all. She just couldn't take the stress of fame and, well, disappeared."

In *A World of Light* May Sarton describes herself as a lyric poet. Most of her poetry is written with a formal structure and rhyme scheme. "Lately," she says, "I've been getting mail from magazines asking for formal, structured poems. We seem to be in the midst of a revolt against free verse. The only problem is that as I've grown older I've stopped being so formal and am now writing only free verse. I seem to have lost the intensity to rhyme.

"But—and this is important—I support myself by writing. I don't teach and I don't have grants. I support myself by writing and I've been doing it for about forty years. Not many people can say that." (1977)

MAURICE SENDAK

In 1812 two German brothers, Jacob and Wilhelm Grimm, published a little book of "nursery and household tales." It was promptly banned in Vienna as "superstitious." Eleven years later the tales were published in England, having been tidied up considerably by the translator, Edgar Taylor, and illustrated by George Cruikshank, who later became the popular illustrator of Dickens' novels. The book was a great success, but the original tales haven't been the same since.

A new collection of twenty-seven of the stories, entitled *The Juniper Tree and Other Tales from Grimm*, is now published in a handsome two-volume edition illustrated by Maurice Sendak, the author of *Where the Wild Things Are* and *In the Night Kitchen* and one of the finest author-illustrators in America. The new translation, except for four tales translated by the late Randall Jarrell, is by Lore Segal, the Viennese-born novelist and author of the children's book *Tell Me a Mitzi*.

Mrs. Segal first became interested in retranslating Grimm into English when she was unable to find an edition she was willing to read to her own children. Every translation she came across was based on some prettified version of the stories. "They were often charming translations," she said the other day, "but the picturesque language put up a barrier between the children and the tales. Also most of the early translations missed the point of the stories, which were originally told to the Grimms by nurses, housekeepers and soldiers in language that was crude and unprettified."

It was only when she read Randall Jarrell's translations that Mrs. Segal found Grimm as she thought it should be. "It is important to remember that the Grimms wrote the stories as though they were being told aloud. All too often this feeling has been translated out of the stories." The one thing a translator of Grimm must do, she feels, is "to maintain the sense of breathlessness of the original German."

Maurice Sendak had long wanted to illustrate Grimm, and although he and Lore Segal together selected the tales in their edition, he was not prepared, he admits, for some of the things he learned from her translation. He was particularly surprised to learn that Rapunzel was the mother of twins. "I was so happy for her." As a result, his drawing of Rapunzel shows a voluptuous, languid teenager, looking as though she had just stepped out of a Pre-Raphaelite painting.

Commenting on his illustrations for the edition, Sendak says, "They are a grand gallery of all the artists I've loved and copied for years." Some of the pictures, such as that of Rapunzel, are, he says, in the style of 19th-century English children's-book illustrations; others are more German, more in the style of Dürer. "They are the most grown-up pictures I've done, the most open and the most personal."

Before beginning the drawings, he visited Germany, examined earlier editions of the tales ("to check up on my competition"), talked with Grimm scholars and looked closely at the German countryside where the tales supposedly are laid. He learned that the first illustrator of the tales was a younger Grimm brother named Ludwig. Jacob and Wilhelm never said much of anything about Ludwig's work, but they greatly admired Cruikshank's. Sendak says that Cruikshank stressed the sheer fun of the tales: "His is the extroverted Grimm; mine is the introverted. There is so much in the tales no illustrator can handle it all."

Maurice Sendak strongly rejects the suggestion that the Grimm tales are, in fact, grim. "If dreadful things happen to you in Grimm you've done something to deserve it. Unlike Hans Christian Andersen, there is no sadism. The stories are all about love and sex and murder—all the things we love. They have now been put back into their original shape, and it's going to be a pleasant surprise for intelligent people. *The Juniper Tree* is a serious book, seriously published"— here Sendak broke into a grin—"and I'll kill anyone who says it should be kept away from children."   (1974)

Maurice Sendak has just received a batch of terrible reviews. They were for a jaunty comic-book-like tale called *Some Swell Pup, or Are You Sure You Want a Dog?*, a book he illustrated and wrote with Matthew Margolis, a professional dog trainer.

"They are the most savage reviews of my career, abysmally negative," Sendak said recently. "I know it's bad form to complain about reviews, but this is irksome. Adults are so hung up on toilet training that they can't see straight. It doesn't bother the kids. They know that puppies go to the bathroom on the floor."

What has outraged reviewers about the book is that indeed the puppy does go to the bathroom on the floor—several times. Other critics have objected to the comic-book format, seeing it as a falling off from the high level Sendak set in his last book, *The Juniper Tree*.

As for the style, Sendak says, "I wanted the book to be as broad and as fast-paced as possible, a small work neatly done that says all I want to say and no more. I had just spent two years doing the drawings for *Really Rosie*, a TV special, and I'd say that *Some Swell Pup* is done in the same style as TV animation. *Juniper Tree* was my watershed book. All my styles came together there and it solved a lot of technical problems for me. I have more control now than ever, but that doesn't mean every book has to be in that style."

Some Swell Pup is the story of a brother and a sister and their new puppy—which they loved until it stopped being cute and started acting like a puppy—and a guru-type older dog who wanders around wearing a long robe and giving sage advice. It grew out of Sendak's own experiences in trying to train his German shepherds. "I was as bad as the kids in the book," he says. "The dogs would drag me down the road. I'd get mad and scream and yell. I think they still wonder when I'm going to go bananas again." What changed Sendak's approach was seeing Matthew Margolis on a TV talk show.

Sendak got in touch with him and Margolis retrained the dogs. Later, when there were puppies, Sendak raised one of them according to Margolis' rules. The two then collaborated on the book.

"You can't blame a puppy for being normal," Margolis said the other day. "They can't be trained until they are ten or twelve weeks old. They chew and they wet. The thing *not* to do is punish them for things they can't help. You have to accept their nature. Consistency, patience and affection are the most important qualities in dog training."

Sendak adds, "I learned I was the problem, not the dogs. I was giving them my anxieties. By controlling myself I learned to control them. Of course *Some Swell Pup* is not a dog-training manual. There are millions of those. We just wanted to set the stage for what to do before the training begins. And of course it is not really about dogs at all; any child could see through that."   (1976)

CYNTHIA PROPPER SETON

Cynthia Propper Seton, who writes her own jacket copy for her books, calls herself "a committed feminist" on the dust jacket of her new novel, *A Fine Romance*. "I'm middle-aged, almost 50," she said the other day, "and I have three names, but I don't want people thinking I'm one of those three-name lady authors. In my lifetime I've been Cynthia Propper, daughter of a Bronx politician, and Cynthia Seton, wife of a Northampton, Massachusetts, doctor and mother of five children. I'm both people, and I'm not going to give up either name."

Her last novel, *The Half-Sisters*, won the praise of many feminists who were not the least put off by her three names. "If you begin as a feminist at 38 or 43 your life has to change," she said. "You can't be put back into the bottle, but I think the women's movement has to realize that there is a middle ground between walking out on your husband and joining Total Woman. If you are married to a louse, get out, but most of us do love and admire the men we live with."

A Fine Romance, a somewhat muted comedy of manners, follows the strains that develop in a marriage when an American doctor and his wife and four children take a winter bus trip through Sicily. The Setons took a similar trip in 1968. "We were the only Americans on the tour, and after a few days the others on the bus seemed to endow us with all the qualities of an idealized family. My husband was turned into the tour's paterfamilias, and we became the walking embodiment of the myth of the happy marriage. We were idealized out of our minds."

When marriages reach a breaking point, Mrs. Seton says, "you should work for your own accommodation within the situation. In marriage, it's insane to ask if you are *really* happy or *really* in love. It is easier to get out of a love affair than a marriage, and at times to lie and cheat in marriage can be more ethical than walking out. I'm interested in the ethical conundrums of decent people, the problems of stable people. The problems of alcoholics or addicts don't interest me because they have already found a way out. I don't want to do research on used-car salesmen or people who live in trailers. I want to write about people I know, about how self-respecting people can become more humane. I suppose you can say that I write comedies in that, at the end of my books, my characters' level of generosity has increased. They are no longer so intransigent."

She acknowledges that her brand of feminism is probably not in the mainstream of the movement. "Every feminist organization I join," she says, "spends the next three years trying to get rid of me. Feminists like me were never like Ibsen's Nora. We always knew we were playing house. It is a way of holding the system together, but we don't want to be taken for granted or looked down on or made to feel guilty. I like housework, but I don't want to be appointed to doing it forever. So, I look for compromise. One reason I'm fond of compromising, I suppose, is that I'm afraid not to. I'm a mistress of the middle ground because the edges scare me."

(1976)

DR. GEORGE SHEEHAN

Dr. George Sheehan will be 60 this year. For the past fifteen years he has been running at least an hour a day. "I can go two days without running," he said recently, "and then I become cranky, irritable and downright obnoxious. Which might be a common complaint with runners. A woman in California wrote to me that she has a poodle that had neurotic sexual habits until she started taking him running with her. If they skip two days, however, he becomes as disgusting as he was before."

A few years ago Dr. Sheehan caused quite a stir with his book *On Running* (described by James F. Fixx, author of *The Complete Book of Running*, as "the book that more than any other captures the magic and majesty of the sport"), and now he has a new book, *Running and Being*, in which he expands upon his philosophy of running, which is to say his philosophy of life. "The first half hour of the daily run is for the body," he says, "the second half hour is for the soul. Joggers—who tend to run because they think it is good for them rather than for the joy of running itself—rarely get to the second half. And it is a serious question whether they should. What you learn there is going to change your life, and you have to be prepared for that."

Running literally changed Dr. Sheehan's life. "It set me free," he says. At 44, he was a thoroughly bored internist in a small town in New Jersey. "Medicine had become an illusion that failed. I had reached the point where I couldn't stand that endless round of patients who didn't really have that much wrong with them, and I had become tired of medicine's emphasis on so-called facts. Facts really aren't very important, you know. The average shelf life of a fact is four years. The reason Hippocrates is relevant today is because he said nothing at all about facts. He dealt in principles and rhetoric. Anyway, I was bored. I had run in college, and I noticed that some of my sons were running every morning, so I gave it a try. From then on everything was different."

He gave up his private practice to become a cardiac specialist, and he began to write. "Writing for me," he says, "is the finished form of truth discovered while running." *Running and Being* grew out of columns Dr. Sheehan writes for the *Red Bank Register* ("I'm on the sports page for reasons the sports editor sometimes wonders about") and *Runner's World*. On days a column is due he usually runs twice as long as usual. "When I run all my circuits open and my stream of consciousness becomes a torrent. Something releases everything I've read or seen, and it is like a great kaleidoscope. Something a high school teacher said or something I saw in an old movie or a paragraph of Emerson's suddenly makes new sense. Like Thoreau, I don't trust a thought I have while sitting down."

Dr. Sheehan makes no bones about his admiration for Emerson, and it is a rare Sheehan essay that doesn't have at least one quote from him. "He's my favorite philosopher, and my favorite Emerson quote is, 'Be first a good animal.' He didn't run himself, but he was a great walker and once walked all the way from Concord to Amherst. He was six-feet-three and weighed 130 pounds and couldn't do anything around the house: a prototype runner. In the last New York Marathon I was huffing up this god-awful hill at the twenty-three-mile point when someone on the sidewalk called out, 'Hey, Dr. Sheehan, what would Emerson say now?' It was the best thing that happened in the race." Sheehan, at five-feet-ten and 139 pounds, thinks he looks like Emerson. "In my old age I've discovered that people I agree with tend to look like me."

He also seems to take pride in his well-honed sense of misanthropy ("I don't particularly wish my neighbor well") and aloofness. "I find no joy in community," he says in a statement that doesn't quite account for his twelve children. "The whole family runs. If they can't play basketball they run, except for one daughter who hates running and demands that part of our dinner conversation *not* be about running. That lasts about thirty seconds."　　　　　　　　　　(1978)

LESLIE MARMON SILKO

Leslie Marmon Silko started writing what she thought was going to be a comic short story about a Pueblo Indian who couldn't be kept on his reservation. When she finished she had a novel, *Ceremony*, about an Indian soldier who returns to his tribe from a Japanese POW camp in the Philippines and finds that his life will never be the same again. "Somehow," she said the other day, "my simple little story turned into the archetypal story of a post-World War II Indian. I'm not quite sure what happened."

Leslie Silko was born in 1948 and grew up in Laguna Pueblo, New Mexico. In her novel she mixes a straightforward prose style with almost chantlike tribal stories and legends. "I grew up hearing stories," she recalls, "both Indian folk stories and historical stories. One of my great-grandfathers was a white who left Ohio in the 1880s; another was a mixed-blood Indian who was pushed out of Oklahoma, after the territory opened up to white settlement, because mixed bloods were hated even more than pure-blood Indians. One of my great-grandmothers was a Navaho and she loved to tell stories about the old Apache raids. Her father had been killed by Apaches on a sheep-stealing raid.

"She used to say, 'If you remember the stories, you'll be all right.' Stories held the people together and told you who you were, but they also had healing qualities. For curing sores on your face, for instance, there were stories about red ants. But most of all, each person carried with him the stories of his family. Even today at a Little League baseball game at Laguna, you might see someone in the stands turn to the person next to him and tell a story about the ancestors of the kid who just got up to bat. And this is something that not just the old people do. Part of who that boy is is formed by the stories told about his family. He knows the stories, and so does everyone else."

When Leslie Silko was growing up in the pueblo, adults spoke Laguna but the young people did not. "I went to a Bureau of Indian Affairs day school, and we were punished if we didn't speak English. The BIA was all caught up in preparing us for a non-Indian world. It's strange because to-day the children are encouraged to learn all they can about their own culture; a complete turnabout has happened in the last ten years."

She now teaches in the English department at the University of New Mexico and lives again in Laguna, in her grandmother's old house, with her husband, a lawyer, and their two children. Her husband grew up in Ketchikan,

Alaska, and most of *Ceremony* was written there. "It's the Alaskan rain forest," she says, "180 inches of rain a year. You have no idea what the effect of 180 inches of rain can be on someone from the desert. My descriptions in the novel of rain in the Philippines actually came from Alaska—all that water was driving me just as crazy as my Indian."

She is concerned, though, that she was not able to write that comic short story about an Indian. "It is so much easier retelling serious Indian legends," she says, "that I think the humorous aspect of Indian life is being overlooked. I would especially like to do something with the traditional humorous stories, which are often the ones that are most prized by Indians themselves. The clowns are the highest ceremonial class in the pueblo, and much of their humor—even in the most sacred ceremonies—is scatological and obscene. As the sacred dancers are doing their most serious dances, the clowns will be their most outrageous, and everyone is laughing. It is almost like laughing at High Mass except you are supposed to be laughing.

"For example, I once worked at a Hopi school, and they invited me to one of their most important ceremonies of the year. It is held in February, when the bean plants begin to sprout. The ceremonial dancing had been going on in the kiva all night. Twelve beautiful young men, the best-looking young men in the village, danced very seriously, never smiling, never looking at the other people in the kiva. Suddenly, up on the roof, there was all this banging around. Someone shouted down at the dancers in Hopi, 'Aren't you ready yet? We're getting horny up here.' And twelve clowns, men dressed as women, with torn panty hose and plastic hair curlers and Halloween masks, came down through the roof and started teasing the twelve serious dancers, who never paid any attention to them.

"That's the Indian's view of the world. You can't have just beautiful men staring into space and acting otherworldly, and you can't have just lewd clowns talking dirty and pinching bottoms. There's room for both, and there has to be balance."

(1977)

159.

CHARLES SIMMONS

Charles Simmons, who lists himself in *Who's Who* as a journalist, published his first novel, *Powdered Eggs*, on his 40th birthday. It won the William Faulkner Award as the best first novel of 1964. "James Joyce," he recalls, "published *Ulysses* when he was 40, and when I hit 39 I had this feeling that I had to come up with something soon."

After the novel was published and the prize won, Simmons' marriage broke up. "For the first time in my life I was on my own, and I began to concern myself with real problems, like clothes and food. I began to see that there was some pattern to the future. Before, the future had just been a dark place to step into. I started writing short autobiographical vignettes. I'd pick a subject, say animals, pets, and begin with my earliest recollections, bring them up to date and then move on into the future. It got so I could turn out twenty of the things a week, and then I was able to start on a novel." Entitled *An Old-Fashioned Darling*, it was published in 1971.

"Writing is extremely difficult for me. I take fifty pages to finish one book review." Which is why, although Simmons has been on *The New York Times* since 1951 and an assistant to the book review editor since 1963, few reviews bear a Simmons byline. "I'd rather use that time writing something else."

After publication of his second book, he returned to the vignette form, and the result is his new novel, *Wrinkles*, all about a writer who published his first book when he was 40.

"As to the obvious autobiographical aspects," he says, "one is embarrassed, but what the hell are you going to do? A novelist's biography is his capital. He has to dip into it from time to time. A friend of mine read something I wrote and said, 'You aren't writing, you're just retelling a story I've heard you tell before.' So I said, 'If a painter does a self-portrait you don't fault him for not inventing the human

160.

face.' I don't think it was a comeback that impressed him much. It's like cooking. If you serve squash you don't just put raw squash on a plate. You do something with it."

What Charles Simmons has done with it is to write one of the funniest, saddest Portraits of the Artist that I've seen in some time. (1978)

ISAAC BASHEVIS SINGER

Isaac Bashevis Singer was out of the country when his latest collection of short stories, *A Crown of Feathers*, won this year's National Book Award for Fiction, an award it shared with Thomas Pynchon's novel *Gravity's Rainbow*.

When Singer returned to New York I had a chance to talk with him in his Upper West Side apartment. It's foolish to prejudge what an interview is going to be like, but I arrived at West Eighty-sixth Street assuming our conversation would be much like other Singer interviews I had read over the past decade: about how he came from Poland to America as a young man and how although he writes in Yiddish he is a truly American writer; about the problems of translating Yiddish into American English; about the sadly ignored state of the contemporary short story; about the probable existence of the devil. Singer usually combines Old Testament wisdom with impish humor, a foxy Jewish grandpa who knows a *dybbuk* when he sees one.

But this time Singer—who turned 70 in July—had something specific he wanted to say and was intent on saying it: "Too many people are now boasting that they don't read fiction anymore. This didn't happen by accident. It happened because they have been disappointed too often by the novels and short stories critics have told them they should read. Too many critics, intelligent men, are calling garbage gold when they know it is garbage. If you need false witnesses for a bad book you can get them by the dozens. In literature and the arts there are more false witnesses than you can find in the law courts."

He went on to say, "The tragedy is that the victims are the good writers. Who cares about bad writers? They always find a way to get ahead. Too many writers are dabbling in sociology and politics, but they can't hold an audience for the length of a book. A good book should have tension and suspense. The fact that there is cheap suspense is no argument against genuine suspense. Poetry has lost its joy these days and its audience. Fiction, I'm afraid, is next. Literature has fallen into the hands of people who are indifferent to literature."

Since Singer has won two National Book Awards, been nominated for more and mentioned by some (Edmund Wilson among them) as a candidate for the Nobel Prize, I asked if this debasement is mirrored in the awarding of literary prizes. "They usually go to worthless books," he said, "because of friendships, politics or the financial needs of publishers."

If all this is true, what should be done about it? "Writers must actively join together," he said, "to organize openly against the commercial praising of junk and to tell readers that they are being systematically lied to about the quality of books. Maybe it can be done through a writers' magazine, I don't know, but voices must start speaking out. If we leave literary criticism to the smearers and false witnesses, it will be a tragedy. Bad taste goes together with bad deeds."

Then with a twinkle in his eye he added, "Of course you must remember that because I speak against smearers doesn't mean I might not be a smearer myself. I used to be on the lookout for angry young men who would speak out, but I've found that they've only been angry with themselves. Now I've decided an angry old man will do." (1974)

SUSAN SONTAG

"What," Gertrude Stein asked in one of her plays, "is a photograph?" Susan Sontag, in her new book, *On Photography*, offers some answers, and the result reads like a wild and brilliant collection of aphorisms. Photography, she writes, "is an act of nonintervention . . . a soft murder." "Photographs, which cannot themselves explain anything, are inexhaustible invitations to deduction, speculation and fantasy." Yet "nobody ever discovered ugliness through photographs. . . . Nobody exclaims, 'Isn't that ugly! I must take a photograph of it.' Even if someone did say that, all it would mean is: 'I find that ugly thing . . . beautiful!' "

Paintings sum up, she writes; photographs do not. "Photographic images are pieces of evidence in an ongoing biography or history. And one photograph, unlike one painting, implies that there will be others." From the very beginning "photography implied the capture of the largest possible number of subjects," its goal "to democratize all experience by translating them into images."

Some critics have taken all this to be an attack on photography, a suggestion Susan Sontag herself rejects. "I don't think photography in itself is an art form," she said the other day, "but putting down photography is like putting down oil or the weather—it is everywhere, a natural resource. I'm not talking about photography in a moralistic way. I'm simply talking about its implications. I have an illness, and its progress is followed by X-rays. Photography, then, is keeping me alive. It is an instrument of power."

Miss Sontag is a novelist, an essayist and a filmmaker, but she doesn't take still photographs. "I'm too interested in doing things well and too hooked on photography to take up picturetaking as an occasional thing. I've been following it all my life, not as a critic of individual photographers (photographers don't interest me that much) but as someone who is fascinated by the subject.

"A photograph, you see, is always perceived as its subject and not as a thing in itself. Of course you can see different styles. You can recognize a particular photographer's subject matter or use of light or the quality of the print itself. But a photograph is always a picture of *something*, and that gives photography a primacy that paintings don't have. Anything can make a good photograph, and that infinitely enlarges the realm of the beautiful."

If she is not a photographer, she is a collector of photographs and of quotations about photography. Indeed, the last section of *On Photography* (the book is unillustrated, by the way) is an anthology of photography quotations that range from Elizabeth Barrett to Marshall McLuhan to recent Polaroid ads. "I'm an indiscriminate collector of photographs," she says. "As a young girl I cut out photographs of World War II from *Life* magazine and pasted them in a scrapbook. They form my oldest memories of public events. But I can't destroy a photograph. I can't tear them up. It's too much of a rejection."

One of her favorite photographs in her collection is a motion study by Eadweard Muybridge, the turn-of-the-century English photographer who made his headquarters in California. "The older the picture is, the better," she says. "Buildings and photographs are two things that get better with age. They become romantic ruins. It is almost impossible to find an old building or an old picture that's ugly. We can't see them as people of good taste in the 19th century saw them, but they are objects of nostalgia in themselves. But I probably can't destroy them because they are magical."

She sees surrealism as lying at the heart of photography. "Surrealism always courted accidents, welcomed the uninvited, flattered disorderly presences," she says, "and it sees reality as being magical. Photography *is* magical, or as close as we can come to it, and it is magic that works. You snap the shutter, and you get a picture. X-rays do tell us what's going on inside the body." (1978)

GILBERT SORRENTINO

Mulligan stew, according to the *Dictionary of American Slang*, is "made of any available meat(s) or vegetable(s)." Gilbert Sorrentino's *Mulligan Stew* is a novel made of available plot(s), character(s), song title(s), publishers' rejection letter(s), you name it, all stirred together in what must be one of the most gleefully self-indulgent books of the year. Any reader who enjoys reading it half as much as Sorrentino obviously enjoyed writing it is in for 445 pages of laughs and bitter chuckles.

In his last book, *Splendide-Hôtel*, Sorrentino observed, "At the moment the artist realizes he has no ideas he becomes an artist." It is a sentiment Sorrentino still subscribes to. Passing through New York on his way to the University of Scranton, where he teaches creative writing, he said, "The only idea in *Mulligan Stew* is the idea of the making of a novel. It's the world of literature, not a photograph of the real world. I can't write in an empty room. I have to be surrounded by books, and I use them.

I can't write without looking things up. You think all that stuff comes out of my head? No way. The literary interview in there, for example, the one with the famous writer, is composed completely of authors' statements pulled out of my files of twenty years of little literary magazines. The whole book is that way, bits and pieces. It's fun, but tough work, and I'm happy if I do half a page a day."

The novel opens with a collection of rejection letters for a book called *Mulligan Stew* by an author called Gilbert Sorrentino. "Twenty-five publishers turned down the book before I took it to Grove Press," says the real Sorrentino, "a place where I used to work as a copy editor. The rejection letters are pretty close to the ones I received, although I added a few touches of my own." In the novel itself, a writer named Anthony Lamont is writing a mystery novel that "employs" characters borrowed from James Joyce, Dashiell Hammett and F. Scott Fitzgerald. The characters all have lives of their own outside the pages of the authors who employ them, and one of them keeps a diary bemoaning his fate of falling into the hands of Lamont. Lamont, meanwhile, carries on his own literary vendettas.

"I keep my eye on trashy literature to see if there is anything new in trashy prose," Sorrentino says, "but there isn't. This season's crop of best sellers, as usual, isn't worth a damn. Reading them is like watching TV, but then so-called great books also bore me to death. I do like Henry James and books in the spook and ghost story trade (especially Algernon Blackwood's), and if I were a scholar I would go into 16th-century lit. I also like Irish writers (my mother was Irish, half-Irish and half-Welsh), men who write brilliant books read by ten people." *Mulligan Stew* is dedicated to Brian O'Nolan who under the name Flann O'Brien wrote *At Swim-Two-Birds*, another novel in which characters get away from a writer to live lives of their own.

"Mostly I'm my own best audience. As I write, I really break myself up. But *Stew* was finished way back in 1975 and I've done two unpublished books since. You hear about the problems of first novelists. But with each book I publish—and there have been about a dozen—I find it harder to get published. This one better sell. The boredom of finding yet another publisher is enough to drive me up the wall." (1980)

WILLIAM STEIG

"**I** used to live in Manhattan, smoke heavily, drink, turn on and draw," William Steig said the other day. At 72, he is looking back on his 50 years as an illustrator and cartoonist. "Now I live in Connecticut. I don't smoke or drink. I have a phonograph but never seem to turn it on. I can turn myself on by looking out the window, and I still draw. The only difference is that I miss Manhattan. Maybe I'll put this place up for sale and move back."

To celebrate his 50 years as a *New Yorker* contributor, he has just published an album-size collection, *Drawings*, which includes work that dates back to 1968.

"I'm lazy," Steig says, "and I won't do anything that I can't sell. I suspect this comes from the fact that I've supported my family—first my parents and then my own family—by drawing from the very beginning. For the past 12 years I've had a successful sideline in children's books. [His *Sylvester and the Magic Pebble* won the Caldecott Medal in 1970 as best illustrated children's book of the year.] Even my attempts at wood sculpture paid off. Nelson Rockefeller bought a half-dozen of them. He got a special price because he got so many, and one of them burned up when the Governor's Mansion in Albany caught on fire."

Steig has published 10 collections of drawings for adults since 1939, not including his illustrations for the psychiatrist Wilhelm Reich's *Listen, Little Man!* (1948). When he was 40 Steig was a patient of Reich's but he rejected my suggestion that the heavily lined faces of many of his worried characters might have come from Reich's theory that repressed people develop noticeable "character armor."

"I always drew that way," he says, "long before I met Reich. In fact, my drawing styles have changed very little over the years. They may go in cycles but the same styles keep coming around again and again. I'm actually more influenced by the kinds of paper or pens I use than by what is in my head. A pen that produces a thin, scratchy line, for instance, will produce a very different cartoon from a pen that makes a fat, heavy line. As for the way my people dress, the idea is that I'm dealing with eternal verities, so I can't have them looking too stylish.

"Years ago I would set out to draw something in particular. Now I'm willing to accept whatever I happen to draw. More often than not I surprise myself, which I suppose makes me more of a real artist."

Steig lists himself in *Who's Who* as a "humorous artist," and I wondered if he didn't like being called a cartoonist. "I'm not fancy," he replied. "What matters is what I draw."   (1980)

JOHN UPDIKE

John Updike is now 42 years old. In the last sixteen years he has published eighteen books: novels, poetry, children's stories, short-story collections, essays. His hair is a bit grayer than his photographs suggest; he speaks quickly and openly, with a hint of a chuckle behind his words, as though he doesn't want his interviewer to take what he says all that seriously. Perhaps because basketball has a way of popping up in his fiction, it is difficult not to see him as a former high school basketball player (which he says he isn't), not the star center but a fast and tricky guard.

Updike and I met in Boston to talk about *Buchanan Dying*, his new book, which is also his first play and his first "historical" work. It deals with the life and death of James Buchanan, Lincoln's immediate predecessor, America's only bachelor president, the only son of Pennsylvania to reach the White House, a man whose motto might well have been "All action is evil."

The play, which Updike refers to as a "reading experience rather than a theatrical experience" (and which might run as long as seven hours if played as written), is dramatically effective not so much because of Buchanan but because of Updike: you keep reading to see what he is going to do next to move the pageant along.

Buchanan Dying began as a novel, or at least as an idea for a novel. Updike grew up in Pennsylvania not many miles from Buchanan's home near Lancaster, and he wondered why, when other presidents were honored by having such things as schools and roads named after them, nothing much was ever done for the local boy who supposedly made good. In 1968, "as an act of penance for a commercially successful novel set in New England"—as Updike slyly describes *Couples*—he began research on Buchanan, which he later continued both at the Library of Congress and in the British Museum. But the project did not seem to get anywhere.

This was, Updike says, not altogether unusual. For every novel he has published there has been one discarded novel. For instance, his true first novel, a "huge" manuscript entitled *Home*, will never be published, he says, and before he wrote *Rabbit, Run* he completed much of a high school novel entitled *Go Away*. Several years later, with the hope of going back to work on it, he read a few chapters aloud to his wife. After a while he stopped and said, "This isn't any good, is it?" She said, "No," and that was the end of *Go Away*.

Updike says that he has found it important for a novelist to choose "not from the heart of his experience but from the fringes. The heart of your life as you live it is soggy. It might make a short story, but not a novel." He has also found that he gets bored writing novels when he gets to the middle. "But writers are like ditchdiggers," he says. "After a certain point you have to keep at it until you get to the end of the ditch."

While Updike was "mired"—to use his word—in *Buchanan* he found himself thinking more and more about his mother's efforts to become a published writer. As a boy he

169.

remembers her working on a book about Ponce de León, a book she is still working on. In recent years Mrs. Updike has published fiction under her maiden name, Linda Grace Hoyer, but Updike says he can vividly remember "that pile of rejection slips, a cliff of unpublishedness." About that same time—Updike thinks he must have been 13—he decided that he was going to be published in *The New Yorker*. "Perhaps I was narrowly purposeful," he says, but ten years later his first *New Yorker* story appeared.

As for being "mired," between the time *Buchanan* was begun and when it was finished, he managed to write *Rabbit Redux* (which contains, as a private joke, a character named Buchanan, a black co-worker of Rabbit's); *Bech: A Book*; a collection of short stories; and a collection of poems.

But Buchanan continued to have a hold over him. "I'm driven to losers rather than winners," he says, "and Buchanan was certainly a major loser." At some point after *Rabbit Redux* was finished, *Buchanan* became a play, and the pieces slowly came together. Both *Rabbit* novels are written in the present tense, as a play is written—a tense Updike discovered useful for *Buchanan* because "it makes you more aware of the moment with no ordering perspectives of the past." And finally it was finished, with such Updike flourishes as the suggestion of a flirtation between Buchanan and Queen Victoria and an entire scene in French—"I've always had a ridiculous compulsion to write in French, a language I don't know."

Currently Updike is finishing a short contemporary novel, and then he will illustrate a children's book he has written—the first commercial illustrating he has done since he was an undergraduate cartoonist on the Harvard *Lampoon*. "Somehow," he says, "I became professional as a writer and my drawing has stayed on the *Lampoon* level." But he studied at the Ruskin School of Drawing and Fine Art in Oxford after graduating from Harvard, and he says that "I used to get so excited drawing that my hands trembled."

Another new development in Updike's life is that his children (he has four) have started reading his books. I suggested that that might sometimes produce some curious looks across the breakfast table. Updike's reply was a chuckle. One of his sons was even assigned to read *Rabbit, Run* in his high school English class, which Updike thought an odd choice. If he had been the teacher he would have assigned *The Centaur* instead.

I said that one of my favorite scenes from an Updike novel was in *The Centaur*, when the boy and his father pick up a hitchhiker who steals a pair of gloves from the back seat of the car. Updike said that seems to be everyone's favorite scene, even Yevtushenko's. After the Russian poet read it he told Updike, "You are a man who could play with giant boulders, but you play with rubber balls."

Then Updike and I said goodbye and he went back to his house on Labor-in-Vain Road in Ipswich.   (1974)

JANWILLEM VAN DE WETERING

"The Dutch have never had much of a military tradition," says Janwillem van de Wetering. "We go in more for individual crime, piracy, gin drinking on the high seas, that sort of thing." He was talking about why he took the option of becoming a reserve policeman in Amsterdam rather than go into the Dutch Army. "I was really a draft dodger, and I thought working evenings and weekends as a policeman would be a great joke. I was in for a great surprise."

He joined the force about sixteen years ago. Since then,

he has given up his career in the textile business and has spent a year and a half in a Buddhist monastery in Japan (his first book, *The Empty Mirror*, was about that). He has also been writing detective novels based on his police experiences and now lives with his wife and daughter in a Zen community north of Boston. He just published his fifth mystery, *The Japanese Corpse*, in which detectives investigate the disappearance of a Japanese businessman in Amsterdam and end up matching wits with the *yakusa*—the Japanese Mafia—in Kyoto.

"The Amsterdam police aren't brilliant, but they're dogged," he says. "Since there are only about five murders a year, they *have* to solve them. Most of the murders involve foreigners. We Dutch are much too boring to kill. But even in Amsterdam, which is the lunatic asylum of Holland, it's really very hard to get arrested. The police are great talkers, they are trained to be, and they'll argue with anyone: drunks, thieves, muggers. People who are aggressive toward police are usually just trying to get the attention of the state. A policeman is the easiest representative of the state to find, and his job should be to find out why they want attention and take out the sting."

Van de Wetering wrote his first book in Dutch and then translated it into English. Now he writes first in English and then does a Dutch version, which is usually longer than the original. "My descriptions are more detailed in Dutch, and I add references to things only the Dutch would know. Also, I have old friends and enemies over there to make cracks about. I snuck my mother into one book, and she recognized herself. I got an angry telephone call out of that."

A character he "snuck" into *The Japanese Corpse* is the Ambassador, who is based on Robert van Gulik, a Dutch Orientalist and diplomat who became Holland's ambassador to Japan in the late 1960s. Van Gulik was also the author of a number of mysteries starring Judge Dee, a 7th-century Chinese magistrate. "Van Gulik was a hero of mine," van de Wetering says. "I never met him, but I went to his funeral. He was a great scholar, and he became a Zen Buddhist."

As for the American phase of van de Wetering's own progress as a Zen student, he says, "I'm hopeless. My teacher —who won't, by the way, read my books—says I'm the pupil who never caught on to what it's all about. But I meditate. It's hard work, but I do it. In Japan I had to do it twelve hours a day, which got pretty painful." He takes delight in the fact that while he is a Buddhist and his wife is Jewish, their 16-year-old daughter plays the flute in the local Presbyterian church. He also takes delight in the friendship he has struck up with the village sheriff. "Except for all his fancy equipment, he's not much different from the men on the Amsterdam force. He lets me ride around with him in his squad car, and last weekend we found ourselves at two o'clock in the morning in the midst of a brawl with seven drunks. It was like the old days."

And the novel he is working on now? It's called *The Maine Massacre*. He has found a way of getting his Dutch detectives to New England. (1977)

KEITH WATERHOUSE

Billy Liar, with his day-dreams of glory and his impossibly botched-up life, is one of my favorite fictional characters, and it is hard to believe that it has been seventeen years since he first appeared in Keith Waterhouse's novel. Now Billy is back in a new Waterhouse novel, *Billy Liar on the Moon*. He's older, in his mid-30s, married, still living in a god-awful English Midlands town, still daydreaming of glory and pretty girls, still making a mess out of his life, still being very funny indeed. He's older, but not noticeably wiser.

Keith Waterhouse is a novelist, playwright and journalist, and he was recently passing through New York City on his annual American tour, gathering news items en route for his column in the London *Mirror*. "The original *Billy Liar*," he said, "has been a novel, then a play, then a film, then a television series, and now it's playing as a musical in London. It's been everything but an ice show."

Was it hard getting back to Billy after all these years? "It took me a while to realize that I was actually writing about him again," he said. "I wanted to do a novel about someone who wasn't properly adult, someone who walks around in an adult's body but who hasn't altogether matured emotionally. I'm fascinated by people who are self-consciously adult, but I'm not all that fond of absolute grown-ups. They're usually far too pompous. Anyway, I was planning the novel— I get an urge to write one about every four years—and suddenly I realized it was old Bill that I wanted to write about. From then on it was easy."

Waterhouse calls Billy "a survivor, even if he isn't a winner." And, he adds, he looks just like Tom Courtenay, who played the part in the movie. "Albert Finney originally played Billy on the stage in London, and Courtenay, who was his understudy, later replaced him. Finney was good, but as soon as I saw that haggard, careworn face of Courtenay's I knew he *was* Billy. That's still the face I see when I think of him."

In the new novel, Billy is working as a minor public relations man for a small market town being leveled under the guise of urban renewal. Misdirected civic improvement is a subject that interests Waterhouse, and the proposed destruction of Grand Central Terminal was one New York story he was writing up for the *Mirror*. "The silver lining of the current economic slump in Britain," he says, "is that they've stopped pulling down old places and started fixing them up instead. The destruction in British towns and cities has been shocking, and it's all being called progress. Until now the preservation movement has been limited to churches and castles. The idea of saving money by actually preserving something in which people can live and work is just starting to catch on."

How much of Keith Waterhouse can be found in Billy? "Not much, maybe 25 percent. We both come from the same part of the country, but I'm a little older than he is. Like him, there are times when I don't feel all that grown-up, and when I light a cigarette I sometimes half expect someone to tell me to put it out, but if I were really like Billy I would have ended up in Wormwood Scrubs Prison long before this."

Unlike Billy, Waterhouse came to London and made his way as a literary jack-of-all-trades. "Sometimes," he says, "I think people believe there are really three or four Keith Waterhouses. There's the one that writes novels and another who collaborates with Willis Hall on movies and plays, and then there's the journalist. People who know me as a novelist never seem to know I'm that columnist on the *Mirror*. My journalist friends never let on that they know I write for the theater or the BBC. But perhaps it is all just a matter of British politeness. I suspect they think it's in bad taste to be more than one thing at a time and are just covering up for me."

(1976)

TENNESSEE WILLIAMS

"The last time my mother saw one of my plays," Tennessee Williams said, "she said, 'Son, I think you ought to find a new occupation.'" He hasn't followed her advice. Since the play she saw, *The Seven Descents* of *Myrtle*, opened and immediately closed in 1968, he has rewritten the play (under the title *Kingdom of Earth*), published a new book of short stories (*Eight Mortal Ladies Possessed*), rewritten the last act of *Cat on a Hot Tin Roof*, written several new plays and just published his second novel, *Moise and the World of Reason*. He is also at work on his autobiography.

Williams quoted his mother when he was visiting in New York while on a trip from his home in Key West to Washington, D.C., where the new version of *Cat* was about to open at the Kennedy Center. His agent said, "Tennessee says that if he has one more revival he's going to feel like Billy Graham." Williams chuckled through his catlike grin and reminded us that his next opening, scheduled for Boston in June, will not be a revival but a new play, *Red Devil Battery Sign*, starring Claire Bloom and Anthony Quinn.

Williams, his agent and I had met to talk about the novel, *Moise* [pronounced Moe-ease] *and the World of Reason*, but it was a subject Williams didn't seem eager to discuss. A short book, full of lyrical monologues, it deals with one night in the life of a young unpublished writer: he thinks about his current, none-too-faithful lover, Charles, and his former lover, a professional skater who called himself "Nigger on Ice"; he attends a party given by a female painter named Moise; and he meets a once-renowned playwright in a Bowery saloon.

I told Williams I thought it was the most sexually explicit work of his I'd read and wondered if the new wave of openness in publishing accounted for its appearing now. His agent said what I had to remember was that many of Williams' plays and short stories once had shock value, and that it is only now "when people aren't being shocked any more that you can appreciate how good they really are."

Williams ignored that and said, "The times have nothing to do with it. I've always written just what I wanted to write. That's why I don't consider myself a professional writer. I tried to stay clear of movie writing in the past because of all the restrictions."

An unusually high number of Williams' works end up in a different form from the one in which they were conceived. Many of his plays were originally short stories. Plays first intended to be one act long turn into full-length productions. *Moise*, typically, began as a short story. How do these transformations take place? *"C'est un mystère,"* says Williams. "Usually I know better how things will end than how they'll begin. So, I keep changing until I get to the ending I had in mind."

His first Broadway-bound play, *Battle of Angels*, closed out of town in 1940, although with characteristic Williams frugality it appeared on Broadway in a different version as *Orpheus Descending* seventeen years later. In an essay he wrote about the closing, Williams quotes the producer: "You must not wear your heart on your sleeve for daws to peck at!"

"That's the silliest advice I was ever given," Williams said the other day. Does he still wear his heart on his sleeve? "Hell," he said, "you've got to." (1975)

GAHAN WILSON

The last cartoon in Gahan Wilson's new collection, *". . . and then we'll get him!,"* shows a small boy coming out of a side street surrounded by monsters, giant cockroaches, ghosts, flying pterodactyls, you name it. In the foreground a seedy middle-aged couple are walking their dog in front of the Evanshire drugstore. The woman says, "Here comes that Wilson boy—all alone as usual."

"Of course it's autobiographical," Wilson said. "There was an Evanshire Drugs in Evanston, Illinois, where I grew up. That's where the neighborhood soda fountain was. It was a great town for kids, a great Halloween town. There were always great debates on Halloween between the kids who soaped windows and those who waxed them. The waxers were the bad guys. Halloween, though, is the best kids' holiday of the year. Christmas is an adult holiday everyone pretends is for kids, and a big deal is made about being good. On Halloween you go out and be bad. And then there's the smell of paper Halloween masks. Who can forget that?"

This is Gahan (which means "rocky field" in Gaelic) Wilson's ninth book. His cartoons appear regularly in *Playboy*, *Audubon* and *The New Yorker*, and his comic strip, *Nuts*, runs each month in the *National Lampoon*. Unlike many of his colleagues at *The New Yorker*, he doesn't disdain the title "cartoonist." "It's a great word," he says. "I studied at the Art Institute of Chicago and later in Paris as an admitted cartoonist. It's what I always wanted to be. The great thing about cartooning is that it is not altogether pictorial or literary. There are two legs and you have to use them both or it doesn't work."

Wilson sees the greatest influences on him as an artist as Paul Klee (for color), Goya, the Prado museum ("the greatest collection of spooky paintings in the world") and the *Krazy Kat* and *Little Nemo* comic strips.

He believes his own greatest contribution to cartoon lore is his werewolf. "It's my pride and joy. Whenever one of my werewolves turns into a wolf, all his clothes become too loose for him. Nothing fits and the poor wolf just looks embarrassed."

Is there anything Wilson wouldn't do in a cartoon? "I don't believe in scary illustrations in books for children. It's unfair. As for adults, they can take care of themselves."

(1978)

YIGAEL YADIN

As biblical verses go, I Kings 9:15 seems unremarkable. A modern translation of it reads: "This is the record of the forced labor King Solomon conscripted to build the house of the Lord, his own palace, Millo, the wall of Jerusalem, and Hazor, Megiddo and Gezer." Yet, according to Yigael Yadin, an Israeli archaeologist, "never in the history of biblical archaeology has so much been owed to one short sentence."

Using the verse as a starting point and information gleaned from the partially excavated city of Megiddo as the basis for a ground plan, Yadin located Solomon's buried city at Hazor, a hilltop between Lebanon and the Golan Heights.

The discovery of a 10th-century B.C. Solomonic city, although dramatic, revealed only one phase in the history of Hazor. Yadin has unearthed twenty-two different cities on the site. Often built one on top of the other, they stretch back 3000 years from a Hellenic settlement in the 2nd century B.C. through a citadel burned by Joshua in the 13th century B.C. to an early Bronze Age nomadic camp. Yadin, probably best known for his excavation of the 1st-century A.D. Zealot fortress at Masada, considers Hazor his major work and has just published a handsome text-and-picture book that documents both the history of the hilltop and his excavations there. It is called *Hazor: The Rediscovery of a Great Citadel of the Bible.*

Professor Yadin was passing through New York recently, and we had a chance to talk about his new book. "I cannot," he says, "imagine a greater thrill than working with the Bible in one hand and a spade in the other. The early archaeologists of this century had something of an inferiority complex about sites they were working on in the Holy Land. They were always trying to prove that the Bible was correct. Now, we can assume it is historically accurate, and we can use it the way Schliemann used the *Iliad* to uncover Troy. And it turns out that the early Holy Land civilizations were very rich culturally."

James Michener used Hazor as the model for the imaginary site of Makor in his novel *The Source*. Yadin says that Michener tried to trace the human parallels within the various cities that occupied the hilltop, while his interest has been to trace the physical connections from city to city. "The problem," he says, "is to find the common threads of all the cities." One common thread is the water supply, another is significant building sites.

Yadin is a great believer in what might be called the actor's school approach to archaeology. "Actors identify themselves with the roles they play," he says, "and I try to do the same. I put myself in the shoes of the people who lived there. When I am looking for the ruins of a palace, I ask myself where *I'd* build a palace. Better yet, I ask the people who live there now." When Yadin was trying to find King Ahab's citadel at Hazor, he did just that—he asked a local farmer, who immediately took him to the western tip of the mound. Why? It was the one spot the farmer knew of where even in the heat of summer there was always a cool breeze. Yadin decided to dig there, and he found Ahab's ruins.

Before Yadin turned to archaeology he was a soldier. Indeed, before he resigned from the Army in 1952 to join the faculty of the Hebrew University in Jerusalem (where he is now director of the Institute of Archaeology), he had served as Chief of Operations of the Israeli Defense Forces. "If it hadn't been for my military background," he says, "I doubt if I would have attempted such a huge project as Hazor."

When it comes right down to an on-the-site problem, Yadin's method is as direct as a military man's might be expected to be: "When in doubt," he says, "excavate."   (1975)

ALEXANDER ZINOVIEV

When Alexander Zinoviev left Russia with his wife and daughter in 1978 on a state-approved visit to Germany, he knew he would never return home. Indeed, a month later he was stripped of his Soviet citizenship. He had previously lost both his professorship—in logic—at Moscow University and the friendship of many of his old colleagues. His crime? A book, a novel, a sprawling, brawling, satirical—and frequently scatological—look at Russian intellectuals and bureaucrats. Called *The Yawning Heights*, it has been published in twelve countries including (in a translation by Gordon Clough) the United States and Canada. He is now a visiting professor of philosophy at the University of Munich.

Zinoviev recently made his first visit to New York and in fluent, if heavily accented, English he commented that what pleased him most about being in the West was hearing reactions from his readers. "I never thought I'd hear about that book from readers." In fact, he never thought he would have a book at all. "When it was published in Switzerland in 1976, its contents were a surprise even to me. Parts of it are from lectures I gave. The section on leadership was actually from a lecture at a military institute that was applauded by generals. I don't know if they were paying attention or not. But I would write chapters and fragments, and I would copy down stories I had told my friends, long stories, little novels. These all, let's say, 'disappeared' and then 'reappeared' in France, where they were all put together and were then published in Russian in Lausanne. Three days after it was published I received a secret copy. A few weeks after that, old friends began to avoid me."

The brunt of Zinoviev's attack in *The Yawning Heights* is taken by the intellectuals. "Russian intellectuals have a terrible problem," he says. "They are comfortable, both physically and spiritually, and what I say threatens their comfort. No matter what you hear, Russian intellectuals have too much at stake in the government to want change."

What Zinoviev has to say is a call for renewed struggle. "Russians are in the same besieged position as we were in World War II. We can accept what's happening and surrender, or we can struggle. With struggle there is hope of change. Here is where I part company with Solzhenitsyn. He has a simpleminded view of Russia in which the good, pure 'folk' are oppressed by corrupt leaders, and that someday the evil leaders will fall and the folk will come into their own. This is stupid. You can't separate leaders from people. Where does he think leaders come from? The folk allow their oppression by doing nothing, and intellectuals who encourage doing nothing only aid oppression."

Zinoviev suspects that more Russian expatriates are in Solzhenitsyn's camp than his own. "While I was still in Moscow, black-market copies of *The Yawning Heights* were selling there for 200 rubles, about $300. After I went to Germany the price dropped to 100 rubles, the same that you have to pay for a Bible. What do you suppose that tells you? I can't give you an answer." (1979)